GUNDOG TRAINING

GUNDOG TRAINING

JAMES DOUGLAS

Line illustrations by Ian Oates

DAVID & CHARLES
Newton Abbot   London   North Pomfret (Vt)

British Library Cataloguing in Publication Data

Douglas, James
  Gundog training
  1. Hunting dogs   2. Dogs – Training
  I. Title
  636.7'52   SF428.5

ISBN 0-7153-8336-1

First published 1983
Second impression 1985

Typeset by Typesetters (Birmingham) Limited
Edgbaston Road, Smethwick, Warley, West Midlands
and printed in Great Britain
by Biddles Ltd, Guildford, Surrey
for David & Charles (Publishers) Limited
Brunel House   Newton Abbot   Devon

Published in the United States of America
by David & Charles Inc
North Pomfret   Vermont 05053   USA

Contents

Breed standards given for the English springer spaniel and labrador retriever on pages 16 and 20 are reproduced by kind permission of the Kennel Club

This book is dedicated to:
Ben, who taught me how,
Bracken, who made me better, and
Gillie, the new challenge

Introduction

Gundog training is an aspect of shooting often shrouded in unnecessary mystery. Those knowing little about it imagine that some very special skills are required, and the novice often imagines some highly complex enterprise. At the other extreme is the owner who approaches the task lackadaisically, with the theory that because the particular breed of dog he has chosen has certain abilities bred into it, there is really little need for him to train the animal at all. Then the result is, of course, a lack-lustre dog which reflects its owner's absence of enthusiasm.

In fact, all gundog training is simply the application of common-sense. Anyone with sufficient interest and patience can train a gundog to a very high standard. Naturally experience helps but, with the aid of this book, the complete beginner should be able to produce excellent results, and in so doing learn a great deal about the dog, its personality and behaviour, while also deriving much pleasure and reward.

As far back as I can remember I was interested in wildlife, and the outdoors. Such interest was probably nurtured by the fact that my parents had always put a great emphasis on owning a motor car (in the days when such things were a rarity) to take us all away from the city of Glasgow, which was our home, and out into the surrounding countryside.

In my early teens I bought a single-barrelled shotgun, after months of saving, and spent many glorious, though unproductive, months wandering around farmland where I had permission to shoot. Quickly I saw the need for a retrieving dog. I could certainly shoot a duck, but it didn't take me long to tire of taking off shoes, socks and trousers to wade into freezing water after my prize! A wounded pheasant that disappeared into long grass necessitated a long search which was usually fruitless. It struck me that this was not only cruel but a considerable waste.

After much persuasion my parents finally allowed me to have a dog of my own; and not as we had had for years, a variety of mongrels which were family pets. Following many more months of saving, I answered an advertisement for gundog puppies (labradors) in a local newspaper. I was lucky in that my first dog was bought with no experience. I simply picked the puppy which appealed the most and proudly took him home. How easily I could have been cheated and ended up with the proverbial 'pup', but fortunately for me the breeder was a man of integrity and he had been selling the genuine article. With the aid of some old books and good advice I gained a super companion which greatly enhanced my pleasure in shooting for many years.

I soon realised how that dog introduced a new dimension to my field sports, for, as with all true field sportsmen, killing has never been an end in itself. With a dog at heel my enjoyment and appreciation of shoots were greatly increased. I'll never forget the thrill when, after long months of laborious training, he retrieved his first duck.

Sadly that first dog is long gone, but others have taken his place. In continuous training over the last twenty years I have never lost my pleasure and I am still thrilled when my experienced working black labrador performs a very difficult retrieve with ease and near perfection. He is a joy to work with and an excellent shooting companion.

Since the first wolf puppy found that cohabitation with man suited his needs, and began sharing man's food and the heat of his fire, so over the centuries mankind throughout the world has formed a special bond with this one group of animals, probably unparalleled by any other. We have used dogs' greatly superior speed, hearing, sight and scent in conjunction with our own higher intelligence to mutual advantage over the centuries. From the swift saluki of the Bedouin that guards his tent and hunts antelope, to the Eskimo husky that lives in fearfully cold conditions, drawing sledges, we have utilised and developed specific characteristics of the various breeds of dog to suit man's needs.

Today, man uses dogs in many different ways, from police

work, shepherding, greyhound racing and terrier work to the group this book is concerned with – gundogs. However, one thing all working dogs should have in common is their enjoyment of what they are doing. Like their wolf ancestors, dogs are natural pack animals, regarding their master as pack leader, and whatever they do, they do it because the pack leader told them to, whether it is rounding up sheep for the shepherd, a police dog catching the fugitive, or the labrador swimming through icy seas to retrieve a heavy goose. All man has done is to refine and develop the dogs' natural abilities. Training one is simply a case of bringing these abilities out, and tailoring them to suit the conditions in which we live. It would, for example, be a thankless and probably fruitless task to try and train a bulldog to retrieve game, for the temperament is wrong and the physique evolved around jaws for crushing, not for carrying a delicate little teal. So we have developed, through strict breeding techniques, dogs which will happily retrieve for us, carrying quarry gently and easily. Training such strains of dog for that purpose then becomes relatively simple and extremely rewarding.

Over the years, what we require of our dogs has changed. In the 1980s most people want more from their dogs. Since most people now can afford to keep only one animal it must be able to both hunt and retrieve, unlike a hundred years ago when the average shooting man had one dog that hunted, another that pointed, and a third to do the retrieving.

Today, with more people wanting to take up field sports and less good shooting land available, we are in the situation of being happy with whatever we can get. We must therefore ask more of our dogs. If our particular shooting ground will yield only two brace of pheasant and a dozen rabbits a year we want to make quite sure our dog will be able to find them and, having done so, be absolutely spot-on when it comes to retrieving them. There is little point in having a dog that will not hunt out that precious pheasant, or that has difficulty finding runners, so today's gundogs must be trained with a little extra care and a little more thoroughness.

It is not necessary to have individual books to train specific breeds – labradors, springers, pointers, etc – since they are all going to perform the same basic tasks, the only difference being that each of them specialises in a particular aspect of the work. The labrador is the ultimate retriever, the springer spaniel the ultimate hunter, and the pointer is the ultimate pointing dog. For the all-round shooting man there can be no better choice of dog than the springer spaniel. However, a mediocre labrador is fine, and usable, whereas a mediocre springer spaniel is a disaster.

If you have a springer or a pointer you can follow this book chapter for chapter. On the other hand if you choose a labrador then put greater emphasis on retrieving work and less on the sections devoted to hunting.

With a labrador retriever you should always keep in mind the important point that if you have any intention of ever trialing ideally its training should be slightly different from that of a dog intended for work. All modern shooting men working a labrador would normally expect him to hunt and flush game, drop to flush and shot, and retrieve. Indeed, the breed is perfectly suited for this purpose, though, as I have already said, is not in the same league for actual hunting as are springers.

But if you intend to run your labrador in trials then it is most inadvisable to allow him to hunt and flush, the reason being that you would greatly limit your chances of ever getting him to work successfully far out from you. In a trial the labrador is not expected to hunt or flush but is expected to be able to cope with long, unmarked retrieves, training for which is dealt with in this book. However, the tendency of any dog that is kept in the close confines of hunting within shotgun range and dropping to flush, is continuously to try to hunt, and you would encounter real difficulties putting him out. You may well get him out sixty or eighty metres, but the dog naturally would be inclined to hunt on the ground. You are asking rather a lot of any animal which has been trained for close hunting/flushing work to ignore all else and keep going out for maybe 200 metres before you place him in the vicinity of an unmarked retrieve, and expect him automatically to zero in. He will have a much greater tendency to hunt wherever you stop him and the further you put him from you the more uncomfortable he will become and will be unsure of himself and your wishes.

Gundog owners fall into two basic categories. On the one hand we have the shooting man with a gundog to help in his sport and increase his pleasure in that sport; on the other there is the predominantly dog man with interests more closely orientated to dogwork, field tests and trialing. In the main this book is aimed at shooting men and it is my earnest hope that in writing it I will have helped them toward a greater understanding and appreciation of their animal.

Much to my wife's amusement I tend to compare the rearing and training of dogs with bringing up children. They are delicate and helpless when tiny, cheeky and playful when a little older, in need of strict discipline during adolescence, but command respect and admiration as young adults. Yet, like children, each dog is different, and will grow and learn at its own pace, some maturing early, others being late developers.

I have based the chapters in this book on a dog's age – three to six months, six to nine months, and so on. If your dog is still on the six to nine month chapter in the book but is ten months, or even a year old, don't get worried, for with your help and patience he will get there eventually. These ages are a general guide only. At all costs do not hurry your dog along before he is ready for the next stage just because he seems to be falling behind. That would be extremely unwise and serve only to frustrate and inhibit you both. He is, after all, just a child, so be patient and success should come.

1

Choosing the right breed

Although an extensive variety of dogs is used in shooting sports it is very important that a prospective owner takes great care in selecting the breed which is most suited to his needs. Unfortunately many inexperienced people are influenced by a friend's dog or the appearance of a particular breed. Admittedly a large part of the success and pleasure in training a dog stems from the owner's enjoyment of its looks, but it does not follow that a dog chosen primarily on appearance will be best suited to the work you expect him to do.

Most people tend to forget that when taking on a new dog they are likely to have the animal for ten to fifteen years, and one simply cannot afford to make mistakes. So before you purchase your new dog you must first decide what sort of shooting most attracts you. There is a considerable selection of breeds available and a look through the 'Dogs for Sale' column in the sporting press might well bewilder the inexperienced. Also, a conversation with any particular breed devotee can be most persuasive. I remember a fellow trying his utmost to get me to buy a Munsterlander, a breed totally unsuited to my requirements. Fortunately I knew sufficient not to be taken in. The decision must be made coldly and in a business-like fashion.

Rough shooting

For the rough shooter who has to work for his game there is probably no better choice than the English springer spaniel. The springer is a hunting dog and the most popularly used of all breeds in this country. It is a great pleasure to shoot over a well-trained springer as it bustles about through even the very thickest cover, ranging around and in front of the gun. A good

springer seems almost able to conjure up game, flushing or 'springing' that which otherwise would go undetected out of the most unlikely corners. While not in the same league as a labrador for difficult retrieves the springer is competent on both land and water, its thick coat and character seeming to make it impervious to even the densest whin bushes and nasty thorn thickets. However, its coat is prone to gathering thorns, twigs, burrs and ticks. Another slight drawback is the dirt and hair it is inclined to cast in the car and on the carpet.

The history of the English springer as a breed is slightly vague, though it is generally accepted that like all spaniels the springer originated in Spain, and was probably brought to Britain by the Romans. Obviously the breed has been refined over the centuries to accommodate the needs of owners, but it was not until the early twentieth century that springers were expected to retrieve as well as hunt.

As with other working dogs the English springer falls into two distinct groups, the 'show' dog and the 'working' dog, and though they are roughly of the same appearance they are not interchangeable. The show dog is bred only for physical appearance, whereas the working dog is bred for its hunting and retrieving abilities. However, as a guide to what a good springer should look like I have included the accepted breed standard.

ENGLISH SPRINGER SPANIEL
Standard of the Breed

Characteristics – The English springer is the oldest of our sporting gundogs and the taproot from which all of our sporting land spaniels (Clumbers excepted) have evolved. It was originally used for the purpose of finding and springing game for the net, falcon, or greyhound, but at the present time it is used entirely to find, flush, and retrieve game for the gun. The breed is of ancient and pure origin and should be kept as such.

General appearance – The general appearance of the modern springer is that of a symmetrical, compact, strong, upstanding, merry and active dog, built for endurance and activity. He is the highest on the leg and raciest in build of all British land spaniels.

Head and skull – The skull should be of medium length and fairly broad and slightly rounded, rising from the foreface, making a brow or stop, divided by a fluting between the eyes gradually dying away along the forehead towards the occiput bone, which should not be peaked. The cheeks should be flat, that is not rounded or full. The foreface should be of proportionate length to the skull, fairly broad and deep without being coarse, well chiselled below the eyes, fairly deep and square in flew, but not exaggerated to such an extent as would interfere with comfort when retrieving. Nostrils well developed.

Eyes – The eyes should be neither too full nor too small but of medium size, not prominent nor sunken but well set in (not showing haw) of an alert, kind expression. A mouse-like eye without expression is objectionable, as also is a light eye. The colour should be dark hazel.

Ears – The ears should be lobular in shape, set close to the head, of good length and width, not exaggerated. The correct set should be in line with the eye.

Mouth – The jaws should be strong, with a perfect regular and complete scissor bite, ie the upper teeth closely overlapping the lower teeth and set square to the jaws.

Neck – The neck should be strong and muscular, of nice length and free from throatiness, well set in the shoulder, nicely arched and tapering towards the head – thus giving great activity and speed. A ewe neck is objectionable.

Forequarters – The forelegs should be straight and nicely feathered, elbows set well to body and with proportionate substance to carry the body, strong flexible pasterns.

Body – The body should be strong and of proportionate length, neither too long nor too short, the chest deep and well developed with plenty of heart and lung room, well sprung ribs, loin muscular and strong with slight arch, and well coupled, thighs broad and muscular and well developed.

Hindquarters – The hindlegs should be well let down from hip to hocks. Stifles and hocks moderately bent, inclining neither inwards nor outwards. Coarseness of hocks objectionable.

Feet – Feet tight, compact, and well rounded with strong full pads.

Gait – The springer's gait is strictly his own. His forelegs should swing straight forward from the shoulder, throwing the feet well forward in an easy and free manner. His hocks should drive well under his body, following in line with the forelegs. At slow movements many springers have a pacing stride typical of the breed.

Tail – The stern should be low and never carried above the level of the back, well feathered and with a lively action.

Coat – The coat should be close, straight, and weather-resisting without being coarse.

Colour – Any recognised land spaniel colour is acceptable, but liver and white, black and white, or either of these colours with tan markings preferred.

Weight and size – The approximate height should be 51cm. The approximate weight should be 22.7kg.

Although on the whole the working spaniel is lighter and more nimble than his show cousin the main difference is in their 'trainability' and desire to work. A working springer need not be unattractive and indeed many are very good looking dogs.

Notwithstanding that the English springer spaniel is the most popular dog for the rough shooter there are various other spaniel breeds which are used for working, though I would not recommend any of them to the first-time gundog owner. Far better to stick to one of the popular breeds; the pitfalls are not so great. Some of the other breeds of spaniel still used in the field are the cocker, the Welsh springer (they look almost like English springers), the field, the Irish (a large, curly-coated dog) and the clumber.

Wildfowling

Serious wildfowling can in many ways make the greatest physical demands of all on a working dog. The fowler expects his dog to be both steady and patient enough to sit for hours if necessary in exceptionally cold and damp conditions, and then find the energy to make some very hazardous retrieves in freezing water. The natural choice for any form of shooting that involves a predominance of water work must be the retriever, and particularly the labrador, for then these dogs really come into their own. They do not hunt as well as the spaniel, and certainly do not point as well as the pointer, but they are absolutely unbeatable at retrieving or finding wounded game. They are, of course, often used for flushing game, though this is not their prime function. They are easy to train and make excellent first dogs.

18

The division of show and working dogs in the labrador retriever is probably more exaggerated than in any other gundog breeds, and I believe this has come about through trialing. Gundog trialing was at one time predominantly aimed at working dogs displaying their abilities in competition, under closely simulated shooting conditions, and the majority of the dogs used in those days were purely and simply working dogs. However, in recent years gundog trialing has become of much greater significance to the human participants. With large sums of money to be earned from puppies and trained dogs the competition is fierce.

The physical appearance of the dogs has actually changed, with a number of trialing labradors moving further and further away from the standard of the breed, resulting in the two distinct types of labrador to be found in the country today. One is the chunky, heavy showdog which emphasises all the best physical attributes and has been played upon by breeders whose main concern is appearance, not ability and brains. The other is the thin, almost greyhound-like trial dog bred for speed and brains to catch the eye of the judge and perform the task in hand efficiently.

I remember once quite innocently asking a friend of mine, at that time a member of the Scottish gundog team, if his dogs were pure labradors! He almost had a fit at my suggestion, yet I really could be excused for my question since his dogs, with their snipe heads, long legs and skinny bodies, did not look remotely like the origins of the breed. He told me that as far as he was concerned physical appearance played no part whatever in his selection. He was interested solely in an animal that could do the job, irrespective of appearance.

There is, however, a third type of labrador and that is the dog which has come from a predominantly shooting background, and certainly may be used for trials, but in the main its pedigree will show a solid working background – some may say humble since field trial winners are usually not too abundantly scattered across such a dog's pedigree. It will have the very desirable double coat and otter tail, so seldom seen in trial-bred dogs.

Remember what labradors were originally developed for! As

water dogs they were required to act as working animals for the fishing communities of the north-east coast of America. They had to swim from boat to boat, or boat to shore, pulling heavy ropes. They were the favourite dogs of commercial hunters, men supplying wildfowl to city meat markets. Such animals needed stamina in fiendishly cold water, thick double coats to keep them warm, and good muscle structure to cope with the heavy demands made on them.

There can have been very few original labrador owners whose top priority was that the dog should whizz across country at high speed. If you took the majority of today's lightly built trialing dogs and asked them to perform the sorts of task undertaken by their ancestors they would quickly show the weaknesses of their development.

LABRADOR RETRIEVER
Standard of the Breed

General appearance – The general appearance of the labrador should be that of a strongly-built, short-coupled, very active dog, broad in the skull, broad and deep through the chest and ribs, broad and strong over the loins and hindquarters. The coat close, short with dense undercoat and free from feather. The dog must move neither too wide nor too close in front or behind, he must stand and move true all around on legs and feet.

Head and skull – The skull should be broad with a pronounced stop so that the skull is not in a straight line with the nose. The head should be clean cut without fleshy cheeks. The jaws should be medium length and powerful and free from snipiness. The nose wide and the nostrils well developed.

Eyes – The eyes of medium size, expressing intelligence and good temper, should be brown or hazel.

Ears – Ears should not be large and heavy and should hang close to the head and set rather far back.

Mouth – Teeth should be sound and strong. The lower teeth just behind but touching the upper.

Neck – Should be clean, strong and powerful and set into well placed shoulders.

Forequarters – The shoulders should be long and sloping. The forelegs well boned and straight from the shoulder to the ground when viewed from either the front or side. The dog must move neither too wide nor too close in front.

Body – The chest must be of good width and depth with well-sprung ribs. The back should be short coupled.

Hindquarters – The loins must be wide and strong with well-turned stifles; hindquarters well developed and not sloping to the tail. The hocks should be slightly bent and the dog must neither be cow-hocked nor move too wide or too close behind.

Feet – Should be round and compact with well-arched and well-developed pads.

Tail – The tail is a distinctive feature of the breed; it should be very thick towards the base, gradually tapering towards the tip, of medium length and practically free from any feathering, but clothed thickly all round with the labrador's short, thick, dense coat, this giving that peculiar 'rounded' appearance which has been described as the 'otter' tail. The tail may be carried gaily, but should not curl over the back.

Coat – The coat is another distinctive feature of the breed; it should be short and dense and without wave with a weather-resisting undercoat and should give a fairly hard feeling to the hand.

21

Colour – The colour is generally black or yellow – but other whole colours are permitted. The coat should be free from any white markings but a small white spot on the chest is allowable. The coat should be of a whole colour and not of a flecked appearance.

Weight and size – Desired height for dogs, 56–57cm; bitches 54–56cm.

Faults – Under or overshot mouth; no undercoat; bad action; feathering; snipiness on the head; large or heavy ears; cow-hocked; tail curled over back.

The labrador is certainly the most widely used of the retriever breeds, though there are others which can be tried. These include the golden retriever, flatcoated retriever, and curly coated retriever.

Moorland shooting

Of all types of shooting in Britain in the 1980s generally the least accessible, both geographically and financially, is moorland shooting, the true role of pointers and setters. The very embodiment of Victorian Britain is a picture of vast moorlands, with the gentleman following his pair of pointers.

Originally evolved for use in conjunction with falconry, the English pointer is the ultimate pointing dog. Unlike most other breeds of gundog the English pointer is extremely independent and will normally work quite happily for anyone.

The other dogs whose true home is on moorland are the setters, both Irish and Gordon. Apart from being used by a few breed enthusiasts in the field, setters are usually found only in the showring today, their elegance sadly taking precedence over the crouching 'set' they were bred to perform.

The all-rounders

The Continentals, with their different shooting cultures, evolved both specialist guns and dogs which were expected to cover the wide variety of game a sportsman was likely to see on any given day. In the case of guns this took the form of drillings (shotgun/rifle combinations) which, apart from being heavy and cumbersome, were designed to cope with anything that came the shooter's way, whether it was a snipe or a pheasant, a stag or a boar.

Now although these guns never really gained any popularity in either Britain or America, Continental dogs have steadily been gaining recognition here over the years, and it cannot be denied that some of the 'all-rounders' have their uses. I believe, however, that generally they are unsuitable for the shooter of the 1980s, requiring more time, space, and attention than is usually available. It is also my opinion that the large majority falls into the category of being jack-of-all-trades and master of none.

The three more popular of the Continental breeds are the German shorthaired pointer (The GSP), the weimaraner, and the

23

Hungarian vizsla, the GSP being the most popular of the three. They are air scenters, unlike retrievers and spaniels which work mainly by ground scent, and certainly have excellent noses, but because of their thin coats they can be unsuitable for working in very cold conditions, particularly icy water. You will always find the individual who will tell you this does not apply to his dog. This normally means that either the dog is exceptional or its owner is not interested in the dog's comfort.

Because of their thin coats these breeds also dislike thick cover. It has been my experience that they are generally too energetic to make good house-dogs, though they do have a gentle nature and seem perfectly happy with all sorts of children and their pranks.

However, shooting over one of these dogs can bring much pleasure as they quarter the ground, find and then point the game, giving you time to prepare for the flush. Yet they do tend to cover a field so much faster than a springer and are really best suited on larger areas which increasingly are becoming rare and difficult to find.

Bracken, a beautiful, working black labrador dog

The labrador is the most widely-used of the retriever breeds

Quiet intelligence, sitting watching. Establishing understanding and control at an early stage of training will lay the foundations for a well-mannered, mature dog

A beautiful springer spaniel puppy, with geese

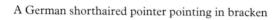

A German shorthaired pointer pointing in bracken

An alert group of English springer spaniels. For the rough shooter there is probably no better choice of working dog

Mrs Rachel Gosling handling five springer spaniels

2

Choosing the puppy

Unless you have already had a dog and are just replacing him, it is advisable to prepare for the new arrival with almost as much care and attention to detail as you would for a new baby. Where is he going to sleep? If you intend to keep him outside you should have the kennel ready for him to occupy as soon as he arrives. It can be unsettling for a young puppy to be kept inside your house when first brought home, and then moved out to a kennel a week later.

The kennel should be warm and dry, and totally draught free, with an outdoor run and a day-board raised off the floor for him to lie on outdoors. If you are only keeping one dog in a kennel you must make doubly sure that he is given plenty of good warm bedding, such as straw, which must be regularly changed. A kennel design shown on page 30 later in the book shows what should be prepared.

If, on the other hand, you intend to keep the dog indoors it is important that his bed area is away from draughts and radiators. Draughts can cause a number of immediate problems – colds, 'flu, etc, and in later years can bring on the horrors of rheumatism and certainly lead to a shortening of your dog's life.

Conversely it is also a bad idea, when keeping your working dog indoors, to allow him the dubious luxury of sleeping beside the fire or a radiator. This can again lead to problems. The animal's metabolism will adjust to the temperature in which he is most frequently kept. In other words, a dog kept in the cool of an outdoor kennel will generate his own body heat. In this way he becomes less vulnerable to cold than the animal which is kept indoors in an artificially-heated environment. The contrast between fireside and icy river can be so great as to make him reluctant and miserable doing uncomfortable work.

As with a child, a dog likes to feel secure from an early age, and by giving him his own bed and bed-place you help to achieve this end, providing a place of retreat which he can identify as his own. If he is going to be kept in the house it is not sufficient for you to arrive home, stick a cardboard box in the corner and expect everything to go like clockwork. What about the puppy chewing the leg of your Chippendale or merrily watering the new Wilton? Nothing is more perfectly designed to annoy your wife and cause disharmony than such easily avoided inconveniences.

Don't buy an expensive new basket. The dog will quickly chew it to bits. Better to wait until he is a little older and past the chewing stage. To begin, an old wooden drawer which is almost indestructible, is ideal, or a stout cardboard box which can easily be replaced. And it is wise, if the dog is to be kept in a hallway, to lift the carpet for the first week or two. At least roll it up at night.

The decision to buy a pup should never be made on the spur of the moment. Enquire among dog owners (if you know any) about availability of pups, and a telephone call to any of the reputable breeders should give you an indication of what is likely to be available. Go along to any gundog trial in your area and ask for advice. Most dog owners will be only too pleased to assist you.

But if these methods are not convenient or possible then peruse the columns of the shooting press which continually bulge

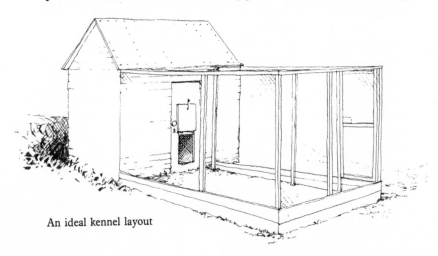

An ideal kennel layout

with advertisements for puppies. However, do not make the common mistake of assuming that if the advertisement says 'keeper bred' or 'telephone Joe Bloggs (keeper)', that this necessarily indicates quality. Some keepers and their methods leave a lot to be desired, and all too often no real selection has gone into the correct matching of the parents.

Regardless of the breeder, with a little care even the novice purchaser should be able to avoid the pitfalls. Before you look at the puppies ask to see the pedigree. There is little point in seeing appealing little playful pups, which few people can resist, set your heart on one and then discover that the pedigree is unsuitable. This can lead to unwise compromise, with the keen prospective owner persuading himself that the dog he fancies will be fine.

When you look at a pedigree, going from left to right, it will start off with the dog's parents, grandparents, great-grandparents and so on. It is of great importance that you get a dog of working strain and you should be looking for the initials FTCh, meaning field trial champion, or FTW meaning field trial winner. However, a word of warning – the initials FTW can also denote field test winner, which is an entirely different distinction, and is no indication of the dog's abilities. Check with the breeder that the initials are genuinely for a field trial winner. Reputable breeders would not stoop to such deception but it is better to make sure nonetheless.

It is the first three generations back from the puppy which will give you an indication as to its future capabilities and potential. It is a widely held belief in gundog circles, which I do not subscribe to, that show winners must at all costs be avoided. Certainly avoid the dog which has show winners closer than great-grandparents, denoted by CW for Crufts Winner, or SHCh for show champion. But if there is the odd show winner from the dog's great-great grandparents backwards, then it is likely that the breeder of the time had specifically bred that blood into the line to improve the dog's general physical appearance.

It is not necessary, nor does it make sense to hold to the ideas held by so many of the field trial fraternity that looks are unimportant. Of course they are important and it is the duty of every serious breeder to endeavour to perpetuate the breed standard. It is possible in all breeds to train excellent working dogs which also look good. But as I have already said, you must satisfy yourself entirely from the pedigree as to the animal's breeding.

Next, ask if you can see the parents. It is not always the case that the sire will be available, but the bitch certainly should be. Examine not only the condition of the dog, but its surroundings. Is it kept in good order? Is the kennel or area where the pups are kept clean and dry? Or is there a liberal sprinkling of yesterday's droppings?

Then you must look at the puppies. Do not dive in among them, but stand back and observe them. Put your arm in beside them and see which one catches your eye. A common opinion is that you cannot choose with any degree of certainty at this stage – eight weeks old – so the choice of which puppy to take from the litter is guesswork, and I have heard of varying methods of choosing, ranging from sticking a hand in blindly and grabbing the first furry body, to letting wife or child make the choice. Nonsense! It is certainly true that at this early stage no one could possibly forecast a dog's future talents, but it is obviously advisable to choose the dog you particularly like the look of. At least fifty per cent of the success of any dog/master relationship must be derived from appreciation of the dog's looks.

You should be looking for a lively, well-set-up puppy which shows confidence, with strong, straight legs, nicely rounded skull and gentle, dark brown eyes. Check that its lower jaw fits neatly under the upper. One that is undershot (with the lower jaw protruding) should be avoided. Another good trait to look for is sufficient self-confidence and friendliness to show no fear of you.

By the time you have satisfied yourself on pedigree, surroundings, and sex, the correct choice of puppy should be fairly easy. If the price is right, buy him, making sure you get your copy of the pedigree before you leave.

The choice of the dog's sex is really a personal one. Dogs are generally larger and more independent than bitches, while

32

bitches are normally more eager to please, easier to train, more affectionate, and can be bred from in future years, but they have the disadvantage of coming into 'season' every six months.

If you go by car to see a potential new puppy it is wise to take a stout cardboard box and an adequate supply of newspapers and rags to bring the pup home in. Pups taken straight from the nest have an unfortunate tendency to dribble saliva, urinate, and quite often vomit. When you deliver him to strange new surroundings keep the family at bay, avoid crowding around him, and supply a welcome drink of lukewarm milk and a little food.

I should also mention that the best time of year to purchase your puppy is early spring. There are several reasons for this. First, you do not have to go to the same lengths to keep him warm as you would in the dead of winter. This is particularly important if the dog is to be kept in an outdoor kennel. The slightly warmer weather also makes the chore of taking a young pup out to do his toilet a little more pleasant (for both of you), and, perhaps most important of all, you will have the long summer evenings to train your dog and bring him up through his most vulnerable period. Since few of us can spend all day training a dog, the after work evening sessions are essential.

Parasites

One problem with a new puppy is that it can be so appealing that it is extremely difficult to keep not only yourself in check but also prevent your family from fondling and playing games with it. You must assume your dog has what I refer to as a 'full house' – parasites both internal and external.

The only person who can really advise you on the treatment and clearance of parasites is your veterinary surgeon. Take his advice, ask him to check your pup's skin for the presence of vermin, and to advise you on the correct treatment for intestinal parasites. Your dog is well protected through its mother's milk against most diseases up till the age of ten to twelve weeks, making the giving of vaccine unadvisable since the antibodies from the mother would prevent a vaccine taking full effect. For that reason vets prefer to inoculate after fourteen weeks. It is a good idea, until your vet tells you the pup is protected, to keep it away from pavements and anywhere other strange dogs may have been.

As your young dog is going to be dependent on you throughout his life to check his skin for ticks, burrs, etc, it is a good idea from an early age to get him used to occasional (preferably weekly) inspections, examining him carefully from head to toe, around the genitals, in the soft folds of skin under the legs, behind the ears, and around the rectum. This incorporated with regular grooming will keep the coat in good condition, free of knots and dead hair. The animal also gets used to, without fuss, a complete 'body search', and means that in years to come your dog will be quite happy being examined, and will not be frightened at unfamiliar probing. Dogs enjoy being groomed and brushed if it is started at a young age and practised regularly.

Worms

The two species of worm which commonly infest dogs are tapeworms and roundworms. Roundworms look like pieces of thin spaghetti with tapered ends, similar to long, thin earthworms, white or pale pink in colour. Most pups are born with these worms already inside them. The puppy will have to be treated for this particular parasite twice, ideally just after you obtain him and then two weeks later. It is imperative that you check with the breeder when you buy the dog if he has been wormed and when. Don't buy worming tablets from the pet shop; you will get a much better result and service from your vet. I would also

Dog faeces with
sections of tapeworm

recommend that you treat your dog every six weeks or so after that, until he is a year old.

Tapeworms can be very long indeed, but it is more normal for small sections of the worm to be seen either sticking around the dog's anus or in his faeces. They are creamy-white and flatter than the roundworm, rather like noodles. They must be treated at once. Your vet will supply tablets for this, and follow his advice. Several treatments may be necessary to eradicate the infestation. You must also be aware that for the rest of the dog's life these intestinal parasites can easily be picked up. You are therefore well advised to treat your dog on a regular, three-monthly basis, and to examine his faeces every so often for tapeworms. An alternative is to feed him a treatment like 'Everfree' in his food. Properly administered it can avoid further troubles.

Fleas, lice and ticks

Ticks can be either grey or reddish-brown in colour and are normally picked up in grass or bracken. They embed their heads into the dog's skin where their bodies become engorged with blood. I have seen some of them grow to the size and shape of a small peanut. Carefully pick off these creatures. It is easy to leave the head imbedded in the dog's flesh, which can then suppurate. Watch the spot so that no infection develops.

Depending on the site of the tick it is sometimes possible to smother it with Vaseline to make it move. Other methods, such as holding a lighted cigarette end to the tick are not

Tick embedded in hair

35

recommended. Your vet can supply you with either a good flea powder or better still canine shampoo to remove ticks.

Mange and other conditions are caused by mites which are too small for you to see clearly with the naked eye. They can cause general skin irritation and infection of the ear, and can usually be cured with a good canine shampoo.

Fleas, as most people know, jump about quickly, are blackish in colour and about 3mm long. Their smaller grey cousins, the lice, move much more slowly. Once again you must assume that your dog can pick these up at any time, and vigilance is recommended for their quick detection and treatment. The problem with this type of infestation is that it can be a devil of a job getting rid of it, requiring thorough cleaning of the house, carpets, etc, complete disinfection of the dog's bedding, or its replacement. The animal will require at the very least two treatments since until all the eggs have been destroyed the infestation can repeatedly reappear.

It may seem that I am biased toward vets, recommending the frequent use of their services, but I cannot stress strongly enough the fact that they are the professionals, there to help you. Their charges are usually modest, and with their guidance you can avoid numerous unpleasant problems.

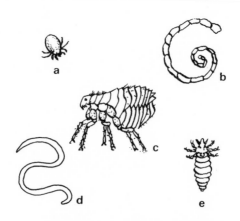

Common parasites: (a) tick; (b) tapeworm;
(c) flea; (d) roundworm; (e) louse

Teaching dropping to shot. Note the pistol behind the trainer's back

Retrieving the dummy to hand

Throwing out the decoy (see top of picture) while controlling three dogs

Inoculations

As I have already said, your vet will recommend and guide you as to the inoculations your dog should have to protect him against the four main diseases likely to be contracted in this country.

Kidney leptospirosis (*Leptospira canicola*). This illness is often missed by the owner of the dog who may have attached little importance to the dog being off colour for a short time, and not realise that the animal has damaged kidneys which can prove fatal. In common with other leptospiral diseases, humans can also pick this up. Therefore the dog must be inoculated against it. This particular strain is carried in the urine and is virulent in cities or anywhere well-used lamp-posts are to be found.

Liver leptospirosis (*Leptospira icterohaemorrhagica*). This is another infection which can be passed on to humans and is a disease of the liver.

Distemper and hardpad. Contrary to popular belief, these are the same disease, but appear in different guises and are caused by a virus invading the nervous system. This horrendous disease, even with modern veterinary medicines, is very serious and normally fatal.

Infectious hepatitis. This has similar symptoms to distemper – listlessness, sickness, diarrhoea, loss of appetite, and high temperature. It is caused by germs infecting the liver.

If you live in the country it is wise after your dog has been fully inoculated that you occasionally take him on the lead around some well-used city lamp-posts. This will have the effect of giving the live virus, with which he has been inoculated, a boost. Actually what you are doing is re-infecting the dog, keeping his protection at maximum.

Should your dog be unwell, off his food, constipated, or you are just not happy with his health, contact your vet immediately. Don't be afraid of being melodramatic for it is better to be safe than sorry!

3

Your new puppy

Remember you have a baby on your hands with no experience or knowledge of anything away from the warmth and security of his mother or brothers and sisters. Expect him to do what feels natural. If he wishes to urinate he will do so. Dry it up; do not chastise him. You could do a lot of damage at this early stage.

When the family retires for the night provide the pup in his bed with an old stone water bottle, or similar alternative, well wrapped in rags, as a heat source to simulate that of his mother. A little background noise of a quietly playing radio or ticking clock will give him some comfort through noise distraction.

If the puppy yodels and yelps you must not answer his pleas for he is almost certainly calling only for attention. After a couple of nights he will quickly learn the futility of yelping and settle down quietly. If you respond to his calls he will get the idea that howling brings results, and your problems will really begin!

A number of canine parasites can live on humans so very close contact between your new dog and your children should be avoided (see previous chapter). Prevent your children from uncontrolled fondling of the puppy as it is easy to transfer worm segments and other bacteria from little fingers straight into little mouths. The problem is of course that many owners gloss over the fact that their puppy is an animal, elevating it to a position somewhere between the animal world and humans. Do not!

Next we must consider the correct way to pick up a puppy. For very young pups, pick them up with two hands, one supporting the stomach and the other supporting the chest. With larger puppies put your arm through the hind legs until your hand reaches the chest, giving the puppy support along his entire length. You then put no strain on any part of the dog's body, particularly his stomach muscles and internal organs.

House-training

House-training your dog is an essential first lesson. It is wrong to chastise your dog for soiling the floor. The best and easiest way to house-train is to take the pup out regularly and often, to the same spot where he 'performed' before. He will quickly recognise the smells of the area and thus be stimulated. After he has obliged, praise him with a pat, saying 'good dog' immediately afterwards, and generally make a fuss of him to show your pleasure.

When the dog is being house-trained make the family aware of the need to watch him all the time. As soon as you see him making the familiar signs, preparing to soil the floor, say 'No' quietly but firmly, take him by the scruff of the neck and pull him to the door, making sure you keep the front paws clear of the floor. It should not be too long before the dog learns to show you that he needs to go out by going to the door and whining or scratching at it.

If the dog persists in soiling the floor, which most do not, then gentle punishment can be administered. It is preferable to shake a dog by the scruff of the neck rather than beat him. Let us imagine you come down in the morning to find a nice pile of excrement on the carpet. Take the dog to the scene of the crime, hold him firmly, point at the excrement and say 'No' several times. Then take the animal outdoors. There is absolutely no point whatsoever in stuffing a young dog's nose into either a puddle of urine or a pile of excrement. That will only frighten and bewilder the dog and set his trust in you back by miles.

In the early stages of your dog's life you must realise that he is a pack animal and *you* are going to take the place of pack boss, leading by example, disapproval, and trust. Most dogs will genuinely want to please you, and if your actions are at all times regular, consistent and quiet you will quickly gain his confidence.

The word 'no' covers a multitude of commands, informing your dog that you do not wish him to continue an action, such as sniffing a teacup on the floor. Care and consideration should be

41

taken. If you put temptation in his way, for instance putting a plate of biscuits on the coffee table, you are inviting him to have some. Therefore think of the dog. Don't rush at him shouting. The word 'no' spoken firmly will suffice.

Naming the dog

It is most important to teach your dog to recognise his name so choose one that is short, sharp and distinctive. Like the simple one-word command, a short one or two syllable name is considerably easier for a dog to hear and recognise.

As soon as you acquire your puppy start using his name at every opportunity, particularly when calling him at feeding times. If he associates the call of his name with food he should quickly recognise the sound and respond to it without hesitation.

Chewing

Chewing can be a most annoying problem in many young dogs, sometimes persisting into early adult life, though normally you will find that after initial teething problems this should disappear. However, do not underestimate the chewing power of a puppy. If you leave your good brogues under his nose expect them to be demolished, or if your wife has just bought herself a pair of expensive leather gloves you can be sure it is these the puppy will ruin first. He will even find the corner of a carpet to work on, so be extremely careful.

At between three and six weeks old your puppy will develop his first teeth, which start to be replaced by permanent teeth from about the fourth month. He chews to help the new teeth through, and you should provide a large marrowbone or one of the proprietary dog chews on the market. These are normally made of rolled and hardened hide, and some dogs enjoy them. Personally I prefer to give bones. Get your butcher to saw one in half, giving the pup access to the succulent marrow. However, your dog may prefer a nice tasty old slipper, laden with your familiar smell.

By giving your dog one or two toys of his own you can generally protect your home, and the chewing should be over by the time he is seven months old. However, a bored animal left for long spells on his own can create havoc, as can pent-up energy, so avoid this at all costs and give regular exercise.

Feeding

The maxim to be adhered to with a puppy of eight weeks is to feed little but often. His stomach is small and cannot handle large amounts so he will need to be fed four times a day at regular hours from the same feeding bowl in the same place. Continue this regime, increasing the amounts in tune with your dog's growth until he is four to six months old, when you can reduce the feeds to three a day.

Suggested meals
Morning Minced or finely chopped meat mixed with a little puppy meal or wholewheat bread, lightly toasted, with a separate bowl of fresh water.
Midday Milk mixed with Farex, Farlene or porridge.
Tea-time Same as midday meal with perhaps the addition of a digestive biscuit broken into it.
Evening This should be the same as the morning meal, eaten about an hour before lights out. This makes the dog want to excrete and aids contented sleep.

Always have a bowl of fresh, clean water, available in your dog's feeding corner where he can help himself.

At the age of four to six months you should feed with three meals daily, dropping the tea-time meal and at the same time gradually increasing the amounts of meat and cereal.

Months six to nine should see feeding reduced to twice daily, with the midday meal dropped.

From nine months onwards your dog can manage happily on one good meal a day, though some people prefer to continue giving two meals, a lighter one in the morning and the main meal in the evening.

The milk ration can be cut down to an occasional treat. I believe that the canine digestive system gets much more use from the enzymes in meat than in dairy products, so the emphasis should always be on meat with a mixture of cereals added.

The amount of food given to puppies varies from animal to animal and breed to breed, and is really applied common-sense. Do not, in the case of labradors or greedy dogs, allow them to bloat themselves until their stomachs are like balloons. The dog's condition will soon indicate over-feeding. Puppies should be plump, not fat. They need quality feeding to help them cope with their rapidly developing bone and muscle structure, and a healthy puppy will be an active one.

Foods
Proteins
Meat should be lean and of any type. Obviously if you are feeding rabbit, hare, chicken, etc, you must remove the bones, and ensure thorough cooking since uncooked game in any form is an invitation to intestinal parasites.
Fish should be lightly cooked by boiling or steaming, and the bones removed.
Eggs One daily, served raw, not boiled as these are difficult to digest.

Occasional macaroni and cheese is inexpensive and very nourishing. Complete dog meal should not be served too frequently.
Carbohydrates Wholemeal toasted bread and dog biscuits.
Supplements I believe that the small additional expense of feeding a dog mineral and vitamin tablets is well worth while. Canovel and Vetzyme tablets supply the B vitamins, Adexoline the A, D, and C groups, and Everfree not only has mineral value but when mixed in the daily food will prevent internal parasites from becoming established.

With cod liver oil follow the manufacturer's instructions on dosage. Remember that just one extra tablet or spoonful of these supplements can be not only a waste, but in some cases detrimental to the dog's health.

Always I try to vary my dogs' meals so that they get used to eating what it suits me to serve – raw or cooked, meat or fish, warm or cold. This discourages the development of strong preferences for one food. Also I encourage my dogs to eat raw vegetables such as carrot or turnip, either by slicing or grating them into their food. Many dogs also enjoy chewing a whole carrot or a piece of apple.

If you feed your dog in the way I have just described he should be happy and healthy for life. Do not get carried away by 'treating' him to chocolate, sweets and sugars. They do him no good at all and can damage his teeth. Instead treat him with a ripe piece of cheese. Don't try and feed your growing dog on the cheap. Remember the golden rule – what you put into a young dog now will determine his future development.

Three to six months old

Up to the age of six months it is important that you do not try to train your puppy, show him off to your friends, or in any other way rush him, putting an old head on young shoulders. During this period the young dog should be allowed purely to develop absolute confidence in both his master and his environment. Through studying the puppy's character and temperament you will be able to lay all the foundation stones on which your future relationship will be based. However, you can start giving a puppy a few easy lessons when he is still quite young.

As soon as I get a new puppy to have confidence in me and feel relaxed in my company I start his early lessons in the gentlest possible fashion, starting with making him sit when being fed. I place the food bowl above his eye-line (which will throw his weight back into a semi-sitting position), put one hand under his chin and with the other gently push his hindquarters down into a sitting position. While doing this repeat the word 'hup'. This is the command to sit. Repeat the word two or three times, holding the dog gently but firmly in a sitting position before putting his food down, saying 'take it' and allowing him to eat.

Your puppy will quickly learn what is required, and there you have it, the very first foundation has been laid.

Many people are surprised at how quickly I can teach my young puppies to sit on command. The beauty of it all is that it is taught easily and painlessly, without either you or the pup being particularly aware of it. Thereafter, when you bring the feeding bowl, holding it in your left hand, raise your right arm fully extended with palm downwards, and say 'hup'. Get him used to both commands delivered together before using the visual one only. As both you and your dog gain confidence in each other you should be able to use the commands separately or together with the same result – the dog's hindquarters firmly planted on the floor!

For the first few months of your dog's life remember to allow him to be a puppy and enjoy his puppyhood. Let him have fun and play with your children, or even have a few toys. A puppy, like a very young child, finds the world a bewildering place and he needs to take pleasure in and reassurance from his 'family'.

On the other hand it is important that you 'dog train' your family. They must be made fully aware that it will be detrimental to the dog's future training if it is always to associate people (particularly visitors) with fun and games. There are conflicting opinions regarding allowing visitors to your home to pet your puppy. I discourage this. While I do advocate demonstrating love and affection to the dog this should be restricted to the immediate family. It does the puppy no good whatsoever to regard all and sundry as potential sources of pats, scratches and fondles. So if your dog is being kept in the house, whenever visitors come in ask them nicely not to touch the dog, other than an acknowledging pat. If the dog then tries for a repeat dose he should be firmly pushed away.

However, conversely the dog can only benefit from love and affection shown to him within the family. If treated in a gentle fashion your dog will quickly gain confidence in the company of strange humans without having the bad manners to make a nuisance of himself. The perfect example of this was at a party in a friend's home. Some twenty people were milling about chatting and laughing, while in the midst of it all his six-month-old puppy, having done its rounds and satisfied itself as to the smell of the individuals, was lying sleeping confidently in front of the fire. It was not cowering in bed in fear, or charging around from person to person having an unnecessary fuss made of it.

So if your dog turns out to be a boring and bad-mannered animal which behaves in an undesirable fashion you must realise that the fault is yours, and your friends. Don't be embarrassed to ask any visitors to your home not to make a fuss of your dog; it will stop future frustration.

Introducing your dog to the lead is a necessary lesson, particularly if you live in an urban environment. I do not recommend chokers for young dogs, a slip lead is better as it is less likely to cause pinching.

When you first put the lead on the dog he will almost certainly plunge and buck. Reassure him by kneeling and speaking to him in a calm, quiet voice. Then try walking forward.

After a few minutes of this take the lead off and let the dog run about. In this way he will soon learn there is nothing to be frightened about and allow the lead to be fitted quite happily, particularly if this leads to something enjoyable such as going for a walk. Whatever you do do not be tempted to use force, you'll only frighten and confuse him.

As your young dog starts to gain confidence in you take him around with you as often as possible wherever you go. Short car journeys will teach him to relax with the unpleasantness of petrol fumes, vibration and engine noise.

When he is used to the lead and confident with you, say around four or five months, a short introduction on the lead to a farmyard (after inoculations obviously) and a walk around the edge of a field of sheep is good for him. Ignore the sheep, and as the dog shows interest in their running, shaking bodies firmly say 'no' and walk on together. But for goodness sake at all costs avoid your young dog going into a field of cattle. They too are inquisitive beasts and will chase after you and your dog to see what you are up to. However, do check with the farmer *before* you march your dog around his yard or field of sheep!

If you are going to let your dog exercise across ground you

suspect may hold rabbits, it is advisable to walk them off before allowing your pup there. Don't be alarmed if he finds a rabbit you have missed and gives chase. It is absolutely wrong for you to chastise him for chasing game at this early stage. He must *never* get the idea that the finding of game is linked with your anger. That can have disastrous results making the dog unwilling to hunt, or retreat at the first hint of game scent.

Early retrieving

Introducing your young pup to retrieving is really simply an innovation in his daily routine of games. Before I go on to tell you how to achieve this it is most important that everyone understands why I place great emphasis on dog-training your family. A wife and children can, out of innocence when playing with a young dog, teach him the most frustrating of habits. The puppy will naturally pick things up in his mouth. Under no circumstances must these be snatched away. This will simply and quickly teach him to hold tighter and play 'tug-of-war', a game all puppies enjoy. Or when he picks up a toy or ball thrown for him, he will run off with it and hide under the table, daring whoever is about to come and play 'chase'.

A dog that is to be taught to retrieve should not be introduced to the fun of being chased, it must always be the other way around.

Don't pounce on the pup every time he picks up a forbidden item, shouting and bawling at him. The result, of that and of snatching a precious 'Action Man' or shoe from him is to make him unsure of having things in the mouth. Therefore it must be emphasised then when he picks up any forbidden item this must be gently removed with no fuss and put out of reach. At all costs do not allow your children to throw an endless stream of balls, sticks or any other item for their own amusement. It will only make a young dog bored with retrieving.

Make a small dummy by stuffing an old sock with a few rags, bind it lightly so that it will fit neatly in the pup's mouth and not trail under his feet. Then when you are next out exercising let him have a run about, and when his attention is on you throw your mini-decoy a very short distance where it can be seen. I have not yet met a puppy which will not immediately run to investigate and pick the dummy up. As soon as he does, crouch down, call his name and encourage him to return to you. He should run straight back to you, where, without removing the decoy from his mouth, you make a great fuss of him.

You do not take the decoy out of the mouth too quickly in order to encourage the young dog, from an early age, to hold game in his mouth until you are ready to take it, avoiding giving him the idea that game has to be ejected as soon as he reaches you. A good retrieve in later life will depend on this, since after all a dog retrieving game that spits it out at your feet is hardly desirable. Gently remove the decoy with much praise. If there is any reluctance in the puppy to give up the decoy very gently squeeze the sides of his mouth between thumb and forefinger. As soon as he has given it up make a fuss again. Put the decoy in your pocket and continue with the exercise period. Under no circumstances be tempted to give him just one more. At this early stage retrieving should be very occasional, say only once every other day.

If when your puppy rushes out to the decoy he picks it up and gallops off with it, inviting you to chase him, do not rush after him calling 'come back'. Turn away and call his name as though *you* are running away from him. As soon as you do that he will of course run after you. When he comes up to you again praise him for coming. If you swear at him for not coming immediately you will confuse him, making him even more reluctant to return to you. Would you run back to someone if it meant being shouted at?

Retrieving must be good fun, a new game. In fact throughout the dog's training all work must be a pleasure or game. Even police alsatians when taught to grab a man by the arm are taught that it is a game. Like any other game the novelty soon wears off if you overdo it, and will quickly lead to boredom.

4

From six to nine months

You are going to require a number of pieces of equipment in the various stages of training your dog and, although in the main their use at this time would be premature, I will list them now since we are going to require one or two of them.

Two whistles – These should be of differing tones, one loud and piercing, and the other quieter and more muted. Avoid the multiple pitch whistles of the type where by screwing them up or down you can vary pitch.

Set of dummies – I have two, of different weights, made of washing-up liquid containers cushioned with rags and stuffed inside an old sock. You can vary the weight by putting sand in the containers. Two is the minimum number you will require and you might as well make three or four at the same time, for use in advanced training work.

Do not use a piece of wood with the rags nailed to it. Wood has little 'give' to it and can encourage the dog to grip hard, and with continuous throwing nails or tacks can work loose and jag or tear your dog's mouth.

Fur and feather dummies – Once again use the washing-up liquid containers, lightly weighted. A little experiment in the kitchen sink will teach you how much weight you require for throwing momentum, while at the same time leaving enough

Dummy made from
washing-up liquid container

buoyancy in the bottle to allow it to float. Put it inside several old socks, bind it firmly and tie a couple of pheasant or duck wings to the outside, or for the fur dummy, a rabbit skin. The idea is to simulate both the texture and consistency of live game.

Blank-firing starting pistol – Available from sports shops.

Dummy launcher – Available from gun shops, or look through the sporting press.

By the time your dog is six to seven months old you can start training him properly. Before you start though it is wise to remember that an untrained or badly trained dog is not just an inconvenience to the owner, but also a nuisance and hazard to other guns. Therefore it is best to strive for field trial standard in your dog. After all, the basic requirements for field trials and general rough shooting are the same – steadiness, discipline, and the ability to find and retrieve game in the shortest possible time.

There are many important factors involved in the correct training of a gundog but none is so crucial as patience on the part of the trainer. This is a point I cannot over-emphasise. It is never permissible to lose your temper and act irrationally with a dog. You must at all times resist the temptation to raise your voice, and if you find you are getting frustrated return home with your dog immediately, until both of you are ready for another try. It is also imperative that throughout the dog's training you avoid boredom or repetition, which will quickly lead to him anticipating your next action. I believe that if from an early age you make the tasks simple and enjoyable you cannot really start too young.

The first part of the training will be concerned with basic discipline – which means that at all times *you will be in control* of your dog. Most bad habits found in working dogs stem from a lack of control at an early age.

You can now start introducing your dog to the whistle. This is easily done at meal times. Your dog will be familiar with household sounds and will no doubt recognise that of a spoon rattling in his feeding bowl! When you are going to feed him call his name and give two short toots on your soft tone whistle. It will not be long before he associates both his name and the two short toots with the same command – to come to you. Then it is a matter of applied common-sense as you start to alternate at different meal times the use of name with no whistle and whistle with no name.

When you are absolutely certain that the dog understands the whistle command to come to you add the whistle command to sit. You have already taught him to sit to the vocal and visual command – 'hup' and outstretched arm. Now start using the whistle too. As you raise your right arm give one toot on the whistle. It should be a slightly elongated toot, like the 'dash' signal in Morse code. The short, sharp, 'dot' toot is a different command, which will be dealt with later. It should not take long before your dog associates the single toot with sitting and will respond accordingly.

When, and only when you are totally confident in your dog's response to these commands within the confines of the home or garden should you take him out to a training area. You should use two or three different areas, alternating in training sessions, in order to prevent your dog becoming too familiar, and consequently bored with the training sessions. Choose an area free of cover and distractions such as livestock or other dogs. Let him have a run about first to assure himself of the scents there and empty his bladder. You should of course have walked all the game off the ground beforehand.

Using your established code of two short toots on your whistle call the dog in. Make a fuss of him and put him in the hup position. Take one or two steps backwards, holding your hand up as in the hup signal. If he tries to get up and sidle after you, return to him and gently replace him on the original spot. Then try walking backwards again.

It is important that you do not peer straight into the dog's eyes. Dogs do not like this as it tends to discomfort them. Either look over his head or at the middle ground between you.

When you are two or three paces away from him make him stay in the hup position for no more than one minute and then return to him, making a fuss of him. Now do it again. Your target is say ten to fifteen paces from him.

When you have reached your position do not be tempted to stretch a good thing. If the dog is sitting don't tempt fate by walking another ten paces backwards; that will come in the future. Ten to fifteen paces is sufficient. Then return to him, again making a fuss. If he tries to come after you at any time as you walk backwards, return him to his original position and make him hup. If he seems to be becoming bored or fidgety, and it will depend very much on the individual animal, it is better to call the exercise off and continue later. But you should be able to hup the dog at least twice and walk backwards to the ten pace mark. Do not immediately call him to you. Let him get used to sitting where he has been put in small doses. Now put your whistle in your mouth and after a few seconds give him the signal to come to you.

If there is any uncertainty or reluctance in the dog to come to you crouch down, making yourself less towering and formidable, and look down. This trick of looking down at your feet when your dog is coming to you will encourage him to come right underneath. Make a fuss of him again, and it is permissible occasionally to give him a small reward. Some authorities disagree with rewarding but I find that the judicious use of a small piece of biscuit or cube of cheese can heighten a dog's interest. There is absolutely nothing wrong with the sensible use of *occasional* bribery. All you must endeavour to avoid is doing it too often or you will quickly teach the dog that when your hand goes into your pocket out comes a biscuit. In addition he can become careless with the task in hand, becoming so eager to get the titbit that he neglects his work. These bad habits should of course be avoided like the plague, but once in every other training session a small reward is fine and certainly aids the establishment of a deep bond between you, while perking up even the dullest of animals.

One of the most important things for you to remember with your dog is always to alternate his training schedule. Never become repetitious or the dog will quickly learn to anticipate your next move, knowing that when your hand takes your whistle to your mouth he is about to be called forward.

Therefore every time you go out for a short training session mix up the order of the schedule. This will result not only in keeping the dog's attention at all times but will also prevent him anticipating and becoming bored. The classic error that most people, understandably, are tempted to make is that when they are getting on well, and the dog seems to be responding so well to training, to just try that one more exercise, that one more lesson. Don't! Short, sweet training sessions are a thousand times better and more productive than two or three long ones. So after each short training period let the dog have a run and then return home.

I should say at this point that your training sessions should be done on a daily basis whenever possible. For most people early evening is the most suitable time of day, particularly during the summer months when the evenings are light until very late. A ten to fifteen minute session every evening is all that you will require. It is pointless thinking you can train your dog on a weekend basis. That would lead only to frustrations and poor performance from your dog. As I said before, the desirability of daily training periods is an important consideration when thinking about the time of year to purchase a puppy.

It is extremely foolish to advance your dog's training too quickly. Take your time, follow the book and make sure that your dog is absolutely capable in each step before advancing. After all, if your seven-year-old daughter was doing exceptionally well at school you would not expect her to be moved in with the fourteen-year-olds. Softly, softly does it – don't try to rush. Too often I have seen the sad results of a dog advanced too quickly. This normally means that the animal has a general smattering of knowledge and eventually control and discipline slip.

Once you have established the regime of teaching the dog to come to the whistle, to sit and stay, it is time to add a short retrieve to the beginning of each training session.

First steps in retrieving

When you first start to give a young dog retrieving lessons, begin by letting him have a good look and a sniff at the dummy so that

A young spaniel learning control, watching the labrador

A young spaniel being sent on retrieve with the older dog waiting his turn

A bold leap into water. If a dog is allowed to build up confidence without being rushed he will almost certainly enjoy this new environment

In mid-air the dog has all his attention fixed on the quarry

he will recognise the smell. I use the smaller of my sock dummies (definitely *not* the fur or feather ones at this stage), and walk him onto the training area, which should be devoid of thick cover, and game.

You will of course allow him a few minutes to burn off excess energy before you begin the day's lesson. Make him hup and then throw the dummy out in front. The dog will almost certainly dash forward to get it. Allow him to pick it up and encourage him to return to you by trotting backwards as I have previously described.

Throw the dummy a second time, but on this occasion squat down beside the dog, holding him gently around the shoulders to prevent another dash forward. Say 'hup' again, and as he steadies praise him. Slowly loosen your grip on the dog until you are gently patting him, praising softly all the while, and then after ten to fifteen seconds send him out, saying 'fetch', pointing with you hand to emphasise the command.

As the dog nears the dummy repeat the word 'steady' once or twice in a calming tone. Later on in the training the dog will know he is near a difficult retrieve when he hears you saying 'steady', so get him used to the word now. When he picks up the dummy give him the recall signal on your whistle, patting your right thigh at the same time, encouraging his return.

Don't assume that your dog will instantly be disciplined enough to perform this exercise on the first day. Every dog's temperament is different. A placid animal may take to it with little difficulty, being more willing to sit quietly waiting for the command to 'fetch', whereas a more nervous, or jumpy animal may have great problems keeping himself in check, being eager to rush out and pick up the decoy. So tailor your methods to suit the dog, and go along at his speed.

Eventually you should be able to leave your dog on hup for half a minute before telling him to fetch, but that may take fifteen lessons to achieve with one dog, and only five with another. Also, don't be a stickler. If this, or any other exercise, is giving problems which are making you frustrated and your dog bored, don't keep returning to it. Forget it for a while, do something else, and when you've both had a rest, go back to the lesson again. You will both be fresh and more able to cope. Remember also to introduce new lessons to your dog at the *beginning* of a training period, when he is bright and eager to get going.

When your dog delivers the dummy to you make him hup and hold him gently under the chin with one hand. This encourages the dog to hold the 'game' high. Now gently take the dummy out of the mouth. Normally this exercise can be achieved fairly easily; however, some young dogs enjoy adding variations of their own to the game. One such involves running around you in a wide circle and keeping hold of the dummy. If your dog starts this, immediately walk backwards encouraging him to come to you, make him hup and remove the dummy from his mouth.

If the dog persists with this gently make him hup, then, allowing a few moments for him to calm down and realise that you are in command, approach him and, putting one hand under his lower jaw, remove the dummy with the other. If he still persists with this reluctance to come straight back to you with the dummy, stop, get him under control, and leave the retrieving for another day.

Your own size and the gaze of your eyes can be most distressing to a young dog retrieving for the first few times. If your dog is reluctant and apprehensive about coming up to you with the dummy try looking at your feet as you encourage him on. Even crouch if necessary, to reduce your apparent overall size. You may find this has the desired effect.

Ask yourself if there might be a reason for your dog being apprehensive of you, especially if he has come back to you without hesitation on previous occasions. He may be frightened of you for some reason, and the blame may not even rest with you, it could have been caused by him receiving a hiding from your wife, unbeknown to you. If at any time you start to lose your dog's confidence, or you wish to regain his trust, feel free, though I must emphasise only on very rare occasions, to produce from your pocket a tasty biscuit. Make a fuss of him and forget retrieving for that day.

There are many other annoying little traits your dog can adopt at this stage. He may stop for a sniff on the way back to you and even drop the dummy. If he does this give the recall signal on your whistle and walk briskly backwards. Stop any further retrieving. Or he may return to you without hesitation, dummy held firmly, but then as he sits he may drop the dummy at your feet before you are able to take it from his mouth. This can be very annoying and is most easily stopped by walking backwards as the dog returns to you, while at the same time encouraging him on with the recall signal. Then, as you make him hup, deftly try to get your hand under his chin. Lifting his head up, gently hold the dummy in his mouth, stroking his head with your other hand and carefully remove the dummy.

Before we move on to the next stage a short appraisal of progress is useful. Your dog should now be confident and competent in sitting down to the command 'hup', the outstretched arm and to the single toot on the whistle. He should be returning to you with the call of his name and two toots on the whistle and should be happy with short retrieves with the hand-thrown dummy. If you have not yet reached this stage do not be alarmed and do not move on. Stick with it, persevere, and have patience, you have nothing but time. Your intelligence is supremely greater than the dog's. Use it. If you have a problem, work out why, and continue trying to solve it until it disappears. Be honest with yourself if things are not going quite right and don't gloss over a problem hoping it will iron itself out because it won't unless you do something to stop it. I have already used the term common-sense in this book and I will continue to use it throughout. At every stage training your dog has more to do with using your common-sense than almost anything else.

Walking to heel

A desirable refinement in any working dog is that he should walk to heel on or off the lead. This is not absolutely essential and should not be too strictly adhered to with hunting dogs such as springer spaniels. Their instinct is to busy about in front of you, and to make them walk strictly to heel will only inhibit their natural talents. It is more desirable in retrievers. I must emphasise that you are not looking for the unswerving obedience one would demand from an obedience school trained alsatian, but really to keep the dog with you by your side, particularly if you live in a city or town.

Take your dog for a walk on the lead. Always keep him in the same position beside you on your left, and whenever he strays jerk him back into position, at the same time saying the word 'heel'. It is in performing this task that a number of people make the mistake of humanising the dog. They allow him a 'little more freedom', letting him roam further and further from the heel position. Always remember that it is *you* in command. *You* are taking the dog for a walk, and not the other way around. A dog taught to walk correctly to heel will be perfectly happy in this position and will have no inclination to do otherwise.

When your dog is used to walking to heel without having to be reminded to do so the next step is to take off the lead. The only aid you should need is a rolled-up newspaper. As you walk with your dog at your side say the word 'heel' every now and again. If he strays from position and the command 'heel' does not bring him back into line a light tap on the nose or backside certainly will.

Your dog should walk at your side when told to heel until you give another command. It should also be sufficient to give the command to heel only once. Keep in mind of course that when you are training a young dog, of any breed, to heel, he should not be made to spend all his exercise time in this position or else the old spectre of boredom may appear again, and a young dog needs more vigorous exercise. I always find it best to make my dog walk to heel until we reach our training field or park.

When your dog is totally at ease walking to heel it is worthwhile teaching him to sit whenever you stop walking, even if it is only for the briefest of moments. In this way you will know that he is always beside you until you give another command. As you walk along with your dog at heel say the word 'hup' when you stop, or blow the 'hup' whistle signal. Do this at irregular intervals and he will very quickly sit, without need of command, whenever you stop.

As I have already said, a busy little spaniel should not be strictly forced with these commands as it is not in his nature to stick like glue to your left leg.

Introduction to water

When you introduce a young dog to water you may be lucky. He may happily go straight in and swim away without fuss. However, do not assume that your dog will fare well in this strange, frightening and dangerous new element. All dogs must be introduced to water with great care. Water is not their natural environment and even the best labrador must learn to develop swimming skills in a variety of potentially frightening situations —weeds tangling legs, exceptionally cold water, water in the ears and trickling down the throat, and so on. It really is a case of taking it easy and allowing the dog to build up confidence in this new environment which almost all of them grow to enjoy.

Choose a warm day and a very shallow pond or gently flowing stream, preferably where the dog can wade, and go into the water yourself, wearing your welly boots. With luck the dog will follow you in and it is quite simple thereafter. Allow him a few minutes' play and then call it off for the day. If on the other hand your dog is afraid of the water, standing on the bank, or running up and down refusing to respond to your encouragements to join you in the water, take him gently by the scruff of the neck, and with reassuring words walk him in beside you, supporting his head. Make a fuss of him in the water and then take him out.

Over the next few visits to the water you can introduce the floating decoy, starting off by throwing this just in front of the dog from the bank. Throw it into shallow water where the dog can wade in to pick it up and return it to you on land. Then the next time you visit the water you can progressively throw the dummy into deeper water, making the dog swim. Do not be afraid that your dog will sink. He will float! Perhaps one in 100,000 animals has negative buoyancy and will sink, and I have never met one. The simple instinct of paddling will quickly teach your dog to have confidence and pleasure.

Quartering

Spaniels and pointers must learn to work, or quarter the ground if they are to develop into useful working animals. This involves careful covering of the ground for game, flushing, or pointing for the gun. Hunting breeds will have a natural ability and desire to quarter, but you must teach control and refine their instincts.

From the outset your dog must learn the methodical working and interpretation of individual scents. Therefore the speed which you work an area will always be important. The last thing you want to develop is a dog which whizzes across the country-side, missing game because you trained him to work too fast. Neither do you want a slow, ponderous animal wandering from scent to scent and keeping you back. The relatively slow walking speed you adopt normally when shooting in cover is the eventual aim, with your dog busying from side to side of the gun.

As with all other subjects you teach your dog, approached in the right way with care and attention, quartering should present few difficulties. Problems only arise from bad advice and, as I have already said and will no doubt say many times throughout this book, lack of patience. Bad advice usually includes a check lead – a long length of rope attached to a collar which you use to control the dog at distance. I have never found this to be of any use. Not only does this inhibit the young dog but also the need to resort to such a curb is an admission of your failure to understand the animal.

Take your dog to a practice area that you know to contain game, especially rabbits, and carefully walk them off. Get your dog from the car and give him a short run to perform his toilet. Call him in to you and take him quietly downwind to the end of the area you are going to work on. Then start forward into the wind so that the dog can discern scents more easily. Walk slowly and tell him to 'get on', indicating you want him to move in front. The dog will naturally bustle forward. As soon as the dog is 15–20m to one side of you give a short, sharp toot on your whistle, the command to turn, and call his name.

As the dog turns to come to you wave your arm in the direction you are going to take and walk in that direction. He will run toward you and pass you. As soon as he does this give the 'turn' signal again, and immediately turn and walk back across in the opposite direction. When you give the whistle signal to turn call his name and wave your arm in the direction you are taking. In this zig-zag fashion walk across your training ground for five to ten minutes. Then call your dog to you and make a fuss of him. Repeat the exercise once more starting at the same end of the training area and working into the wind.

Eventually you should be able to walk forward in a straight line leaving your dog to do the quartering, turning to the toot of the whistle.

If your dog starts taking a line in front of you, following what will almost certainly be a hot, fresh scent, give the recall signal on your whistle, and when he is nearly back to you wave him out and, walking in the direction you have indicated, continue your quartering exercise. This is vital as once again it is a case of you insisting that the dog complies with *your* commands and does not go off on his own accord.

If the dog is shown patience and consistency he will very quickly adopt this pattern of working in front of you. But be careful. Any sloppy behaviour from you will automatically be reflected in the dog losing his pattern. This is particularly true if you have a tendency to walk too fast. In his desire to keep in front of you his criss-cross pattern will become smaller and more uneven until he is more or less walking in a wiggly line.

Once your dog has adopted this new skill it is then time to start 'dropping' him occasionally in mid-exercise with the word 'hup' alternating with the whistle command to hup. When you do this approach the dog, give him much praise and then re-commence the quartering exercise. Do not be tempted to hup him too often, for this will instil uncertainty, making him unsure of your wishes. So just one interruption in every training exercise should be sufficient.

You will find that on some days your dog will be less keen and vigorous than usual. This will almost certainly be due to variations in scent caused by changing weather. I cannot give you any clear guidance on when scent is most likely to be best. Looking over my own notes there is little to indicate when scent may or may not be reduced. However, generally any weather extremes cause scent to dissipate. Warm, dry weather seems to be particularly bad, and scenting conditions can also vary according to the time of day (see section on scent, page 84).

Once when I was shooting pheasants on a particularly dry, hot day, I dropped an old cock which was a runner. My dog, which was very experienced and didn't normally make mistakes, saw the bird fall and I had him away very quickly. He was only a few metres behind the bird when the cock nipped through a fence and into deep cover. It had disappeared. My dog had no idea where the bird was. He sniffed like a vacuum cleaner but couldn't take a line. My companion joined me and put his own dog to work, but we never found that pheasant.

On another occasion I was out with a friend and her beautiful field trials champion labrador dog. I was shooting pheasants in a root field and the dog was to retrieve for me. I shot my first bird of the afternoon and the dog marked it easily. On instructions from his handler he whizzed across the roots, cast about in the area where the pheasant had fallen and tally-ho'd on! Pheasants leapt out in all directions, completely out of range. If the dog didn't find the fallen bird I had little hope of getting another for he had flushed them all!

Eventually the dog found the pheasant, not 15m from where I had seen it fall. Still alive, it had tucked under a root. Obviously scenting conditions were bad that day for two days beforehand the same dog had won an important field trial. The owner's comments were priceless – 'He must have been blowing out when he should have been sniffing in!' But it does show that even the best dogs can be put off by poor scenting conditions.

Ideal scenting weather, and therefore the ideal time to work your young dog, is during the early morning, before the heat of the sun dries the ground out, when everything is fresh and the grass sparkles with dew.

5

Nine to ten months

Steadiness to the dummy

Total steadiness to the hand-thrown dummy is absolutely vital. It is one of the load-bearing foundation stones which must be laid with care. The dog should be able to take commands from you even when you are not standing beside him, and bring the dummy to you.

Make the dog hup, walk 10–20m out in front of him, raise your right hand while at the same time repeating 'hup' or give the whistle command and throw the dummy out with your left hand. If the dog makes the slightest attempt to jump to his feet and run forward, hup him again. If necessary walk up to him and gently but firmly move him back to the original sitting position.

Then repeat the exercise, telling the dog to fetch the dummy. If by any chance your dog ignores you and rushes out to the dummy, ignore his indiscretion and take the retrieve in the normal fashion. Do not continue that exercise any more that day and the next time you wish to try it go closer to the dog before throwing the dummy. You should find few problems with this exercise as it is one which most dogs at this stage in their training have little difficulty in mastering.

Next, stand to one side of your dog, make him hup and fling the dummy well out in front for him to retrieve. You should find that adding these exercises to the training schedule will give you an increasing pleasure in your dog and a sense of real achievement.

Now comes a little variation which many people neglect, yet I feel it is a vital part of the training programme. By now your dog will, if he is at all bright and alert, have started to go beyond just keenness to rush out and pick up dummies. He will have started to anticipate your commands. You may find, for instance, if you make any vocal noise resembling in pitch the command to 'get on' or make a sudden arm movement like scratching your head, the dog will be away out in front of you, off to get the dummy. In other words the dog will have begun to assume that every decoy thrown is his property, representing the fun of a retrieve.

It is at this point in the training that you should start to retrieve every second or third thrown dummy yourself. There will be more of this particular exercise later in the book when I cover all the advanced retrieving with decoys. But start now.

Once the dog has the whole business of steadiness to the thrown dummy firmly in mind you can leave him in the hup position and, after flinging the dummy out, allow the usual quarter minute of just sitting, and then walk out yourself to make the pick up. Return to your original position keeping your dog on hup throughout. A great number of future problems can be avoided by this gentle learning now. The dreaded crime of 'running in', which in later years can ruin so much hard work and pleasure and make your dog virtually useless, can be traced back to the animal regarding all falling game of any kind, decoy or live, as his own property.

But whatever you do throughout the whole exercise of teaching your dog steadiness to the dummy, behave quietly and with confidence, and don't rush ahead too fast.

Jumping

Competent jumping is another requirement in a good working dog, and certainly all dogs have some natural ability to jump over obstacles. However, I would suggest caution in bringing out this ability. If you have a handy stone wall which is not too high you can use this for the exercise. Approach it with your dog and tell him to hup. Climb over yourself and walk on calling to the dog 'over'. He will naturally jump the wall, and as soon as he reaches the other side tell him to hup again and make a fuss of him. Then walk on together.

Barbed wire must not be jumped. I once saw a very pretty bitch leave a nipple neatly embedded on a barb, and torn stomachs are common. So if you come to a barbed wire fence with your dog either lift him over or put him through as I am about to describe. Smooth wire fences should also be avoided. A dog's back leg can easily slip under the top wire and catch on the second wire. The dog's momentum can either break or dislocate the leg. Several times I have seen one of the best of all jumpers, the roe deer, caught by the back leg in a similar fashion, and this can be very dangerous.

So when you approach a wire fence call the dog to you and push one wire down with your foot, pulling the other up, creating a larger gap. Gently encourage the dog to go through. He will quickly learn to come to you and go through the space provided. Later on you will cover advanced jumping over high obstacles, and into water, but at this stage in a dog's life – around nine months old – it would be folly to ask him to go over anything other than the most simple of structures. The dog hasn't yet developed the adult muscle structure. Bones and capabilities are not fully developed, and he is still learning. You should restrict wall jumping to two or three per walk.

You can, however, help to strengthen the leg muscles, particularly in the back legs by encouraging the dog to run uphill. Don't overdo it to begin with, but gradually make him run up progressively longer and steeper hills. But what is the best way to achieve this if you are not a fitness freak who enjoys bounding up mountain sides? Well, the simplest way is for you to stand at the top of a slope and throw a decoy downhill. Obviously the act of retrieving the decoy to you makes your dog run up the hill. Give him two or three uphill retrieves like this, but be careful not to overdo things. Don't over-exert your dog by asking the impossible, especially in warm weather. An over-worked, exhausted, over-heated dog is just as likely as you to have cardiac failure, and most dogs are so eager to please their master that they will literally work themselves to death for him.

Introduction to shot

Introducing a young dog to the sound of the shot is another task which must be approached with great caution. A foolish or careless action now can create very real difficulties by instilling in your dog a fear which can so easily be avoided. Dogs' brains are extremely limited. If they are frightened by a particular action or sound they will always associate it with fear and respond accordingly. Witness firework night. On 5 November every year newspapers, television and schoolmasters throughout the land warn children to consider their pets because such loud and unfamiliar bangs can cause real terror in an animal which after all has no appreciation of what is coming and doesn't know they are just fireworks. A loud bang represents something strange and frightening, and having been frightened once the dog will always associate that bang with terror. So, do not be carried away by the fact that your young dog is 'bold', and be tempted to skimp on the preparation of introducing him to shot.

It is best to ask a friend to assist you, and you will need a starting pistol. You should both go out to the training ground and give your friend the starting pistol. You stay with the dog, make him hup and squat down beside him, comforting him through your closeness. When your friend is about 50m away from you he should be able to fire the pistol safely. At that range it should not frighten your dog at all. He may even give little indication that he has heard it! So far so good. Let your friend come in slowly, firing the pistol at 10m intervals.

Observe the dog's reaction. You may be lucky and your dog will have no reaction to the sound whatsoever. However, from

25m away your friend should come in, firing the pistol at 5m intervals while you make sure your dog is not alarmed. If at any time your dog starts to show distress, stop immediately, change the subject and go on with the rest of his training programme. You can go back to the starting pistol another time.

Gun nervousness

Flinching at the sound of the shot, or gun nerves, is brought on by giving the dog a fright, normally through a gun going off unexpectedly too close to a young dog, or natural caution at the loud bang and fear of the unknown. This problem can be overcome simply the next time you take the dog out by keeping your assistant at a distance when he fires the starting pistol while you stay with your dog, giving him comfort and confidence, and showing him there is nothing to be afraid of. Each day bring the shot closer as I have previously explained. You can also help the dog to get over gun nerves by giving him the odd biscuit immediately after the shot is fired. This will take his mind off the shot. However, as I said before, the use of edible inducements must be kept strictly to a minimum.

Gun shyness

If your dog is gun shy I am afraid that is a very different kettle of fish. This is an inherited problem which you will not have been aware of before this stage, and generally it results in the dog just not coming to terms with the sound. He will either cower beside you or, more commonly, bolt well out of harm's way, or even worse – run all the way home. If you have a gun shy dog I strongly advise you not to keep it, even if it has virtually become a member of the family. You are only making a rod for your own back since as a gundog it will be absolutely useless and could never achieve anything like its potential. If you sell such a dog, do not sell it as a gundog but advertise it as a house pet, and as an added precaution to prevent an unscrupulous individual or someone unwittingly breeding from the animal in the future, do not pass on its pedigree. But if you do I suggest you write neatly across the corner of the pedigree the reason for selling the dog, and sign it.

Unfortunately there is no way you can find out before this age if the dog is gun shy. Do not be tempted, under any circumstances, to move introduction to shot to an earlier part of the training, to save yourself time. That would be most foolish as you could irreparably damage an otherwise competent gundog.

Whistle control at a distance

There is really no reason why you should not be able to control your dog as far as he can see and hear you, yet all too often trainers allow a sort of magic barrier to develop, and once the dog has gone beyond this he is out of the handler's control. This is particularly common in shooting dogs trained by the man who has no experience or intention of trialing. Yet controlling your dog at a distance is not only exceedingly desirable but comparatively easy to teach.

Your dog will now be totally familiar with the commands to hup vocal, upraised arm, and whistle, individually or as a combination of all three, so the following lesson should be learnt easily. When you are going through your training programme you will of course at some point make the dog hup. Ask him to hup by raising your right arm, call 'hup' and then immediately give a toot on your loud whistle. He will sit as he has been programmed to do and should not take long to associate that one loud note with the action from a distance away.

With this incorporated into the daily schedule you should find that after about a week you will be able to drop the hand signal and on the whistle signal alone the dog should hup. Over the next few weeks, on progressively extending the distance between you, the dog should naturally drop to the whistle, even with his back to you. You can then use your loud whistle for all distance controls, using the soft tone one, and the spoken word, only during close work. However, do not be tempted to overdo this exercise. Once in every training period is sufficient, and when

71

the idea is firmly in the dog's mind you should be able to drop him at considerable distances without difficulty.

Dropping to shot

When, and only when you are quite sure that all the training to date, and particularly dropping to the whistle, has been firmly learnt and understood, should you move on to dropping your dog to shot. Take him out to the training ground and put him through a normal training programme. Also take your starting pistol. Your dog will of course be entirely confident with the sound of the starting pistol so when he is hunting the ground in front of you give the hup command on your loud whistle and fire the pistol immediately afterwards. The dog will sit to the sound of the whistle, and through practice another command to drop will be added to his extensive repertoire, that of the shot.

Again I must emphasise that each of these commands must follow in the order they are set down in this book and be learned perfectly before moving on to the next, or else the dog will be completely confused and you will have to go back to square one. Make sure the dog drops to the whistle absolutely automatically before you think of moving on to the shot, and if you have trouble with this or any exercise examine the problem working your way through it slowly and methodically. Persevere with your dog and with patience he will get there in the end.

We have now reached the point in your dog's training where I would stop contemplating any new lessons for a couple of weeks. Continue the daily workout but allow this period to consolidate, and give yourself the opportunity to check each individual task, making sure that each is not only understood, but also being performed crisply, cleanly, and quickly when you give a command. Each time you take your dog out work him through all the training, giving both of you a rest from new techniques.

Your dog should now walk at heel on or off the lead, hup to whistle, hand, and shot, at close quarters or at a distance. He should stay where he has been put when you throw out a dummy, and retrieve dummies to hand both on land and in

Bracken scaling a very high wall

A labrador in characteristic hunting crouch

Clearing a fence in good style. All dogs have a natural jumping ability but this should be developed with caution

water. He should be confident in the water and enjoy swimming. He must come straight to you when called vocally or with the whistle. He should quarter in a pleasing, naturally rhythmic pattern (particularly spaniels and pointers) and show complete lack of concern at the sound of a shot. He should jump small obstacles encountered naturally and, most important of all, he must be within your total control at all times. Once you have achieved this standard the whole training programme starts to become much more interesting.

I have always been horrified at the large number of shooting men who have got it into their heads that a well-trained dog is neither applicable to nor desirable for their particular type of shooting. This is of course utter rubbish and anyone who allows his dog to take on any of those dreadful faults such as running in, chasing hares, etc, should really be ashamed of himself. I have repeatedly been told by way of justification for a dog being unsteady that this is desirable when shooting under certain wild-fowling conditions. It should never be the case that your dog is out of your control at any time. If it is, something has gone seriously wrong.

6

Ten months to one year

Further water work

By now you should have a very good idea of the temperament and preferences of your dog. I find that most dogs particularly enjoy water and therefore this is where I normally start this period of training. For this you will need three dummies, so make yourself another one from washing-up liquid bottles with rags and sock covering as I explained before.

Take your dog to the water, make him hup on the bank and throw the first decoy well out into the water. Make him stay where he is for perhaps twenty seconds and then give him the command to fetch. Take the retrieve, praise the dog, and ask him to hup again. Throw the second decoy onto the far bank where he can still see it. Then after a short wait send him on his retrieve. After the second retrieve throw the third decoy into some light waterside cover, preferably on the other bank, where the dog can see it fall but not actually lying. Once again, after he has sat in the hup position for a short time, tell the dog to retrieve.

It is not usually a good idea to use the same dummy more than once in a day. They may look identical to you, but each one will have an individual smell to your dog. This may be a small detail but I do like each retrieve to be fresh. This can make the difference between enthusiasm and staleness.

Advanced dummy retrieving

Now we come to the point of introducing your dog to advanced dummy work. Take him out, as you have done in all your previous training programmes, and give him a retrieve with the familiar sock dummy. On delivery make him hup again and then throw your fur dummy out. Ask the dog to retrieve. Normally this goes without a hitch and the dog will retrieve as before, but it may be that this new texture of dummy will cause him to stop and play with it. If your dog does this you should, on the first few occasions you send him for the fur dummy, give him the recall whistle as soon as he picks up the dummy, and run back a few steps to encourage delivery to you.

The object of the exercise is to get the dog's mind on coming straight back to you. When he delivers the fur dummy take it and give plenty of praise. Give no more retrieves that day and continue with the rest of the training.

Over the next few days, as your dog gets used to picking up the fur dummy, start throwing it into light obstacles such as long grass and rushes, progressing to small walls. But at this stage always let your dog see where the dummy falls. Blind retrieves will come later.

After your dog has mastered the fur dummy you can introduce him to the feathered one, but wait at least six training sessions before doing this. Use exactly the same tactics as you previously employed. Make him hup, throw out the fur dummy, make him wait, ask him to fetch and take the retrieve. Make him hup again and throw out the feathered dummy. After a short wait tell him to fetch. As with the introduction to the fur dummy, if you think the dog is hesitant, as soon as he reaches the feathered dummy and picks it up, give the recall and run backwards. When he has delivered the dummy to you make a fuss and continue with the rest of the schedule.

Over the next six or seven training periods, or longer if your dog requires it, alternate fur and feather dummies until he is absolutely confident with them. Remember there is no rush. If your dog requires further attention, give it.

Directional hand signals and 'go back' command

Once you are certain that your dog has mastered the various points dealt with so far you can make his retrieves more difficult. This is largely up to the individual dog and owner, but could take the following form. Throw the decoy into long grass or shrubbery where it cannot be seen, though your dog will have observed the direction in which you threw it. Send the dog out for the dummy, remembering to repeat the word 'steady' as he gets close. Progressively throw the decoy further and deeper into bushes, making the dog use his nose as well as mark by sight. This is where the scent of the rabbit skin or wings tied to the dummy will help the dog tremendously.

If at any time the dog returns without the decoy send him back again. Only when it is obvious that the dog cannot find the decoy, when, for example, it is up in the branches of a bush or has fallen underwater in a ditch, go with the dog, find the dummy and let him see it. Then give him one or two simpler retrieves to regain his confidence.

When you are confident and assured of his ability to mark the decoy by sight and find it by scent in tall grass you can move on to directional commands. This is essential for the future career of your dog whether he is to be a field trialer or just a good working dog. For this you will need two decoys. Take the dog into the training field, put him in the hup position and stand about 2m in front of him. Throw one decoy out to the left, about 15–20m from you. Throw the second one out to the right. The dog's natural instinct will be to go for the last dummy thrown. It is important that at all times you impose your will and desires on the dog, so with a clear and concise arm movement and the command to fetch wave the dog out to the first decoy. If the dog goes for the opposite decoy blow the hup command on your whistle and return him to the spot where you originally told him to hup. Wave him out to the first decoy. If, however, he does not stop when you blow your whistle, or has reached the decoy before you stop him, take the retrieve and make no fuss of the dog. Make him hup, collect the second decoy yourself, move on for another 40m or so and repeat the whole exercise again.

When the dog brings the correct decoy take the retrieve, praise the dog, walk with him back to his original sitting position and wave him onto the second decoy. Slowly, as each training session progresses, increase the distance between you and the dog and

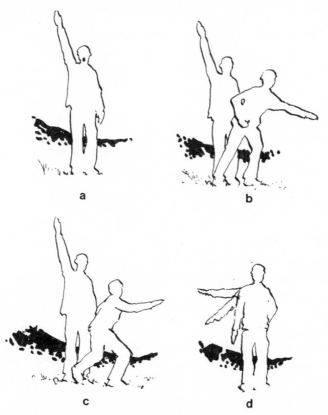

Hand signals: (a) hup; (b) hup, then go left or right; (c) hup, then silhouette is viewed from side for go back, as you reach forward pushing the dog out; (d) bringing dog to you, arm moves up and down

the distance of the thrown decoys, always giving clear signals of a full arm movement – as if you were marshalling an aircraft – when you wave him out. Eventually the dog should be able to take hand signals at 100m, retrieving first one decoy to your hand, then going for the second on command.

The 'go back' command is a simple variation on the theme of directional hand signals. On entering your training area, take a dummy and, making sure the dog sees it, throw it or just drop it behind you. Walk on for 15–20m and make the dog hup. Standing in front of him (facing the direction you have come from) with your arm fully raised and with a downward motion toward the dummy give him the command 'go back'. If he doesn't understand, or has forgotten about the dummy, make the dog hup again and pick up the dummy yourself. Walk further on and repeat the exercise, though making him hup only 5m from the dummy.

Some people advocate sitting the dog facing you and lobbing the dummy behind the dog when teaching the 'go back' command. I do not recommend this, as anything landing behind the dog will necessitate him turning around to see where the dummy is going, and force the dog to stand up.

The 'go back' exercise should be comparatively easy for your dog to understand. It is just a case of adding it to your daily work schedule and lengthening the distance you leave the decoy before asking the dog to go back. You can now vary your retrieves, giving your dog one 'go back' and one forward, or two forward and one 'go back' retrieves, and so on.

As soon as your dog has the idea of 'go back', stop sending him back the way you have come, and change your tactics slightly so that the dog learns that the command 'go back' and the hand signal mean that he should go further back from where you are standing. Go out on your own and throw a decoy into some light cover. Then with your dog approach the decoy into the wind, and make the dog hup facing you. With your arm straight above your head wave it forwards, with the command 'go back'.

The phrase 'go back' can be ambiguous for some handlers. In this context we are actually referring to going back behind the dog, or further back, and not back the way you have come. When you wave the dog out, he will run into the scent of the hidden decoy, his head will go down and he should find it quite easily. If there is a danger of the dog running past the decoy you should blow the stop whistle, and then when he is sitting watching you give him a directional hand signal to the right or left. By increasing the distance of these straight out, blind retrieves as your dog's age and abilities progress you should soon be able to put him out at quite considerable distances, signalling stop if at any time he is uncertain and waving him back on to the right line. You will find that when sent back some working dogs will run 50m at a time, stopping and looking back to the handler for the next hand signal, while others will busy their way out until they either get a whistle signal to stop, or hit the scent, whichever comes first.

The variations and progressions of advanced retrieving work are virtually unlimited. For instance, after making your dog sit beside you, throw your two decoys as far as possible. Leave your dog and walk 100m away. Call him to you and make him hup. Then send him for first one decoy and then the other. Use your imagination, add a third decoy. Any variations you can think of to involve the dog using both mind and memory are good, and you should both be enjoying these exercises.

All this work bears fruit in the field. Let's assume your dog is off the line when going for a bird which he has not seen drop, or which you have seen scuttle off, and you know the dog is not likely to find it himself. At the toot of your whistle you can make the dog hup, and a directional hand signal will indicate the direction he should go in to find the game. The rapport that you and your dog can build up in this exercise is very gratifying, culminating in the sort of understanding I have with my dog. Like many experienced working dogs he will, if confused, stop and look back at me for directional assistance, underlining the contact and team work which both of us have strived to achieve.

Use of the dummy launcher and blind retrieves

Up until now we have been keeping the sound of the shot purely as a command to hup, and separate from decoy retrieving. But now is the time to start putting it all together, simulating the actual sequence of events when going shooting.

With your dummy launcher take your dog into the training field. Make him hup, and fire the dummy launcher. Send the dog for the dummy, using hand signals to show the direction. Do this two or three times, each time allowing the dog to retrieve the dummy and helping with the direction if the dog seems completely lost. It normally takes a few such retrieves before your dog realises that a shot asking him to hup is followed by the sailing into the air of a decoy which he will be asked to retrieve.

He will quickly learn to look for the direction of the retrieve when you fire the launcher. Once he realises this you can take him into long grass or shrubs and fire the decoy into light cover.

However, it is not absolutely essential for you to use the dummy launcher for this exercise. You can easily throw the decoy by hand while at the same time firing a shot with your starting pistol. But you will not be able to throw the decoy as far, and one of the advantages of using the launcher is that it makes your dog get used to seeing a 'retrieve' in the air without the throwing movement which he is used to.

Your dog should now be able to mark and retrieve decoys to you with little difficulty. Once again, if you have taught your dog his lessons carefully and patiently he should have no problem combining the skills from each.

I believe that you should not seriously start blind retrieves until your dog has thoroughly mastered marking retrieves and hand signals. When he is ready, go over your training area without the dog and hide a few decoys. This can be done when you walk the game off your ground prior to a training session.

Put your dog out, let him work in front for a few seconds and then fire a shot with your starting pistol. The dog will of course have seen nothing fall and so will be working completely blind. Using hand signals direct your dog into the wind and on to one of the hidden decoys. It is very important that the dog is worked into the wind with blind retrieves as he is completely dependent on his nose, apart from your overall directional signals, to find the hidden decoy.

Use your imagination with this exercise and hide your decoys in various, though natural, places. Remember always to throw them and not place them by hand since then your own scent would lead straight to the decoy, and don't become over-zealous, putting decoys on top of hay bales, etc, unless of course your dog has wings! Keep your decoys on the ground!

The ultimate blind retrieve is of course one in which the dog is put out to find a decoy without a shot being fired. This is where your control of the dog will be tested severely. Work your dog out into the wind, telling him to fetch and give hand signal directions. When the dog is approaching a decoy remember to repeat the word steady to aid him further.

After he has successfully completed a few blind retrieves he will know what is expected and should cause few problems. Remember to try a few water retrieves as well, for he will probably need to do a lot of water work in the future.

If you are having some trouble with this part of the training, try to discover the cause for concern. If the dog is not dropping to shot quickly enough then you will have to practise that again. If he is not following your hand signals it is either because these are not clear enough or because you were not thorough enough when he was learning to use them. Perhaps he is having difficulty in finding a decoy he has not marked as it fell. Therefore he is not using his nose properly, relying more on his eyes. In that case make the retrieves more smelly – try tying week-old socks to your decoys, and work a little closer to them. Usually no problem is insurmountable.

I have kept the next exercise to the end of the hand training since it is imperative that your dog is quite certain of all commands before embarking on it. As I said earlier in the book your dog should not anticipate commands and become unsteady in the process. What you must avoid at all times is your dog getting used to being put in the hup position waiting for your command, assuming that any sound or movement from you is meant for him. You may be only coughing or swatting a fly when you discover your dog has, out of uncertainty, misinterpreted your action and moved!

A good exercise is to get the dog used to you making noises and actions which are nothing to do with him, teaching him to distinguish the magic one from the meaningless. Imagine you are in a field shooting with a friend. You put your dog in hup and point at something in the distance, saying 'look at that, John', and discover that your dog whizzes off in the direction you have indicated!

How I handle this exercise is quite simple, and causes my friends great amusement. I put my dog in the hup position, walk about 50m in front of him and do a little jig, waving my arms about, singing 'tra-la-la-la-la'. The dog will often look at me as if I'm demented, more often he will stand up uncertain of whether or not I am about to call him in. The instant he does this I stick my arm in the air and command him to hup, then continue with my one-man panto. After each little jig either call him to you or walk back and give him a pat.

Another variation is to leave the dog in hup and go for a walk. Walk away from him and then around your field in a zig-zag fashion, varying your pace, walking, running, standing still, always keeping your eye on the dog, ready to hup him if he moves. But do not walk any further to one side of the dog than a position from which he can comfortably watch you by turning his head. Go behind him and he will naturally get up and turn around.

Yet another variation is to put the dog in hup, walk 50m away and hide somewhere you can see him but he cannot see you. At first give him twenty seconds and then re-appear, unconcerned, walk back to him and praise him. The wait can be extended until you are perhaps hiding for as long as several minutes. The dog will progressively gain confidence and steadiness in being left alone with the knowledge that you will always come back for him.

Scents and scenting

As your dog will now be using his nose with some expertise you should be aware of scenting conditions. It is obviously going to help you throughout your dog's working life if you have an understanding of scent and its variations.

Scent is one of the most important means of communication in the animal kingdom. Most animals use scent to mark their territories, dribbling little drips of urine on lamp-posts, trees, and so on. Some, such as roe deer, have on different parts of their bodies scent glands which they rub on trees, rocks and posts to mark the perimeters of their territories.

Farley Mowatt, the brilliant Canadian writer, tells in his wonderful book *Never Cry Wolf* of how when he was studying wolves in northern Canada he had pitched his tent very close to their den, and right beside the track the three resident adult wolves trod daily when they left to go hunting. Farley had been aware of their use of urine for territorial marking so he decided to carry out an experiment. One day when they were away from the den he marked his own territory by urinating in a square around his tent. The wolves' path came through his square so he urinated across it, and then lay in his tent to observe the animals' reaction.

Later the same day when the large male pack leader returned, Farley described how the animal came trotting down the track until it came to the urine line right across its path. The wolf stopped and cautiously sniffed its way around the edge of the square until it arrived at the track where it came out of the marked territory, and proceeded on down it, quite unconcerned! After that, and throughout the rest of the period Farley was there, the wolves trotted down the track, around the outside of his 'territory', and back on to the track. They were respecting his marked scent territory.

There are two ways in which scent is carried, in the air and on the ground. The smell given off by any particular animal is mainly its species smell. You can, for example, quite easily smell the difference between say a rabbit and a goose. But as in humans it also has a more personal smell, due to its condition, whether it is clean, dirty, a breeding female, an old male and so on. Just as a woman may pass you in the street and leave a trail of perfume in the air, so animals leave their personal smell behind.

Once I had to transport two undesirable characters less than a mile in my car. Neither their clothes nor themselves had probably been washed for many weeks, and after they got out of the car it was some time before the stink disappeared. In other words they had left a strong scent. In the same way, to a very keen nose these individuals would have left their smell in the air as they walked by. The period of time it would hang there would then depend on the air conditions. In hot weather rising air currents would help to dissipate it and in windy conditions the smell would be diluted fairly quickly.

Ground scent can be a mixture of lots of little smells, and

generally speaking ground scent should linger longer than air scent. The type of ground contributes to this scent, whether it is grass or plough, soft, baked dry or damp. You will also get traces of an animal's smell where it has brushed against vegetation, or you may even get the smell of broken grass shoots, bracken or twigs as their internal sap is released and smells very slightly. The 'educated' nose can interpret such information.

Much more important is the animal's scent on the ground as it runs across a field. If you drag a dead rabbit it leaves a distinct scent along the grass, making it easy for a dog to follow.

That a dog can distinguish the smell of wounded game and follow its scent, ignoring the scent of others of the same species which may have also crossed the ground, is to do with a group of chemicals given off by skin glands and indicating emotional condition. (It can also be aided by the smell of blood.) We have all heard the old wives' tale that a dog knows if you are frightened of it. It is true! You are actually giving off a peculiar scent of fear. Equally an animal knows when you don't like it or you intend to do it harm.

Many years ago I watched a dog, some distance away, killing lambs. I knew the dog and who owned it. I shouted to the dog in the distance and it ran off home. Two hours later I called at the owner's home to tell him of the crime. When I arrived the dog was lying asleep in the sunshine. The owner listened to the story with his dog lying happily at his feet. Being the Sabbath day in the West Highlands the gentleman asked me if I could return the following day and shoot his dog for him.

When I arrived the following morning that dog, which had

shown not the slightest concern before, knew something was wrong. It was taken out on a lead, for all the world like a condemned man, no doubt aware of both its owner's distress and my intent. I will never forget the look on that dog's face when its lead was tied to the fence post. That is the sort of animal reaction that is easily put down to human imagination, but in fact there is affirmed scientific reason for the dog's behaviour. It had picked up the scent I was giving off and while I would not claim that the dog knew what was going to happen, it had a good idea that whatever it was would not be pleasant.

Let us say, for instance, that you shoot a cock pheasant which falls dead to the ground in cover. Your dog will go out and, following up the wind direction which will carry the smell of the dead pheasant toward him, the retrieve should be fairly easy if the weather is right and it is not blowing a howling gale. Let us, however, imagine that our cock pheasant has fallen lightly pricked, and is a runner. The bird is frightened and intent on escape. It is therefore adding to its own usual smell the skin glands' chemical secretions known as pheromones. Bleeding will heighten the smell, but runners seldom leave blood over the first few yards. Altogether then the bird leaves behind a distinct trace of its passing, and this scent can linger long or dissipate quickly.

Wind is important in carrying scent. On a blustery day scent will be difficult to follow as the wind blows it in all directions. Just stand next to a camp fire on a windy day and you'll know what I mean. Best conditions are a light breeze blowing in one direction. You would then work your dog upwind, so that the wind will blow the scent down to the animal.

7

One year to eighteen months

Bringing out the gun

Up until now your dog has been working to the starting pistol but this has a different sound from that of the shotgun, being a sharp crack rather than a loud, flat boom. So, like anything new your young dog is to be introduced to, it is better to err on the side of caution than rush in, possibly to regret it later. Exactly the same technique is to be employed as used when the dog was first introduced to shot.

Go into a field, and with the aid of a chum make your dog hup. Stay with the dog as your friend goes about 50m away with the shotgun and fires a shot into the air. If all is well your friend should advance in 10m intervals, firing a shot, until he is 10m from you. If your dog makes any sign of alarm or discomfort, stop, and start again another day, advancing the shooting more gradually. However, any dog who has shown no sign of discomfort with a starting pistol is unlikely to develop anxiety at this stage, though it is certainly better to be safe than sorry. From now on at every possible occasion carry your gun with you throughout your training sessions, intermixing dropping the dog to shot with both shotgun and starting pistol.

Once your dog is responding to your satisfaction it is time to start a close simulation of a day's shooting. Use a method similar to that employed when you taught him blind retrieves. Hide a few retrieves in assorted cover, say one by a riverbank, one in long grass, and one in a thicket. Then working your dog into the wind toward a hidden decoy load your gun with cartridges which have had the shot removed. This is easily done by running a sharp knife cleanly around the end of the cartridge, allowing the shot to spill out. Remember the wad. It can inflict serious damage so always fire your gun in the air, empty cartridge or not.

Work your dog up to where you know you have stashed a decoy, then blowing your hup whistle signal, swing the gun up and fire. Both sounds should make the dog hup. It may seem excessive still to be using both commands, but if you think about it, it is really better to be doubly sure, and at this crucial stage in your young dog's training, when he is beginning to show the benefit of training, it is easy to credit him with more obedience than he really has.

After your dog has been sitting for a short time send him out with the command to fetch, repeating the word 'steady' as he approaches the decoy. Then in exactly the same fashion work your way on to the next hidden decoy. During this exercise it is absolutely imperative that you watch your dog all the time, making sure that he works his way through his entire repertoire.

Introduction to cold or dead game

If you have adhered strictly to the advice given so far in this book you should now be the owner of a well-behaved, skilled and valuable working dog, which needs to add only a few refinements to the training already given. It is at this stage, and only at this stage, that your dog should be introduced to real game – dead first, live later. So far the dog will have been familiar only with decoys tied with skin or feathers. Now is the time to introduce him to the much greater temptation of strong smells and moving targets.

The first thing to do before introducing your dog to dead game is to make sure that any blood is neatly sponged off since the last thing you want to happen when a young dog goes to pick up his first dead rabbit is to give him tasty blood on his tongue. This can put some dogs off, while others performing similarly might stop to lick the game before delivering it to the handler.

If the game you are using is a rabbit in the breeding season, another good tip is to inspect the rabbit's ears. Should there be heavy infestations of fleas on the rabbit's eartips it is wiser just to cut off the tops of the ears. Although you will never completely overcome the flea problem this little precaution is sensible.

Of course it is better to plan ahead. You will have known for several months beforehand that you will need a dead game supply so try to secure a number of snared rabbits to deep freeze. They should be uncleaned and in plastic bags. Obviously if you are using frozen bunnies then make quite sure that they are thawed out before using them as decoys. A hard, semi-frozen rabbit is nothing like the softer fresh one and cannot be pleasant for your dog to carry in his mouth.

Pheasants, ducks, partridges, and some of the smaller hares (but definitely not large hares at this stage) are all perfectly acceptable for this exercise. The weight and bulk of a hare can give a young dog unnecessary difficulties, and a fundamental principle in any exercise when training a dog is to make it as easy as possible. You can of course eat the practice game afterwards, since all you are doing is taking it from the freezer the day before. You might as well skin the rabbit and eat it as it should not have been damaged in any way.

One bird to avoid at this stage is the pigeon. This should not be introduced until your dog is experienced on game as anyone who has shot pigeons will know. Pigeon feathers are extremely dry and loose, and it is particularly distasteful for a young dog to run out keenly, pick up a pigeon and end up with a mouthful of feathers which are difficult to spit out.

Retrieving through decoys

Nearing a goose in water

Practice through reeds gives confidence with tangling roots and weeds

Typical pose of the labrador, the best of all dogs for water work

When you introduce your dog to dead game the same technique as in the introduction to the fur dummy can be used. At the start of the training schedule make the dog hup, then you throw the fur dummy, and put the dog out to retrieve. Take that retrieve and throw the rabbit out in its place. Again put the dog out to retrieve. Do not be alarmed if when the dog reaches the rabbit he has a sniff of curiosity. Give the recall signal and run back a few steps, calling the dog's name in encouragement. Take the retrieve, praise the dog and put the rabbit in your game bag.

It is not a good idea to use the same dead specimen for more than one retrieve for it will already have the dog's saliva on it, and because it has its own individual smell the dog would very quickly know it was the same beast. This can encourage the dog to play with game. He should regard his function on a retrieve as bringing game straight to you and then forgetting about it. If your dog tries to jump up at your game bag to have a sniff, firmly tell him 'no'. Do *not* be tempted to use the same game twice.

Of all the dead specimens available to you rabbits are the prime choice, being of handy weight and size, more easily obtained and less precious than pheasants. If like me you are fortunate in having a ready supply of bunnies hopping around your door, then you will obviously be able to use freshly killed game which is preferable to the frozen variety. Hang your rabbit in a cool place until it is cold before you use it, and do not use a rabbit that is any older than one killed on the previous day. Its smell will be completely different from that of fresh game as its intestinal gases will have blown up.

Introducing your dog to cold birds is equally easy, as you use the same techniques. However, use your head. If you are going to ask your dog to retrieve a dead cock pheasant it is wise to pull out the long tail feathers, thus giving a small dog less chance of tripping over the tail when retrieving. Also limit the size and weight you ask your young dog to collect.

Do not expect him to manage a goose until he is much more experienced for the weight is difficult for an inexperienced dog to manage, and the bulk of a goose body is such that a young dog can end up nipping it by taking too small a grip on the bird.

Then the skin will tear, or the feathers come out, and the dog will drop the bird. This encourages the dog to take a much tighter grip when he picks it up again.

The long wings of a goose are almost guaranteed to cause problems. Later on, when the dog is really experienced, he will, when picking up heavy specimens, naturally hold his head higher, to balance better and keep the wings from under his feet. It is also wise to remember that one of the most aggravating of dog 'crimes', that of a hard mouth, is normally brought on by the dog being introduced to an insecure retrieve too soon.

Taking a line

Almost all dogs have the natural ability to follow a line of scent from an early age. If you are out of sight that is how your puppy knows how to find you, but a little help from you will develop this more quickly. Once again, a little forethought and imagination is all that it takes.

Get an old fishing reel and a length of line. I normally fix the reel to the butt section of an old salmon rod, but in fact a broom handle with a couple of eyelets tied to it will do the job equally well. Make a slip knot on the end of your line and fasten it around the hind legs of a dead rabbit. The reason for this is that you will be dragging the carcass through the grass, and in doing

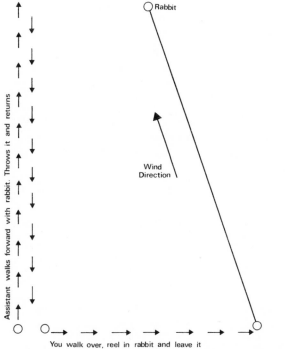

Rabbit

Wind
Direction

Assistant walks forward with rabbit. Throws it and returns

You walk over, reel in rabbit and leave it

so you will be pulling it against the lie of the fur, causing more abrasion and giving a marginally stronger scent.

Enlist the help of a friend and get him to walk downwind carrying the rabbit attached to the line, about 20–30m from where you are standing with the fishing rod. Your assistant should then throw the rabbit to one side and return to you along the same path as he went out. Using the rabbit as a fulcrum and keeping your fishing line fairly taut, walk in a wide arc around the rabbit until you are about 30m away from where it was thrown. Reel it in, untie it and leave it in long grass (if possible) at the end of the 'trail'.

Get your dog and work him into the wind, starting about 50m from where you know the 'trail' starts. As the dog nears the beginning of the trail he should give the tell-tale signs of being onto a scent, such as increased sniffing, tail wagging, or a general increase in activity. You should know your own dog's habits by now. As soon as he reaches the beginning of the trail, fire a shot with your starting pistol to make him drop. Give him a few moments in hup, then send him out to fetch, taking the retrieve in the normal fashion. Over the next few weeks you can increase the distance you ask the dog to follow a line, eventually progressing to about 100m.

Another method of laying a trail, and which requires no assistant, is to tie your length of line around the rabbit's body and walk downwind with it to the point you want the 'trail' to start. Throw the bunny about 20m to one side, paying out the line, and then walk to the other side of the rabbit and reel it in, making sure its scent line is not going to cross over your own. Then work your dog on to the rabbit as I have previously explained, and always into the wind.

Live game

When your dog is accustomed to dead game you can acquaint him with live animals. I have seen more dogs fall foul of the crime of coursing than you would believe. In one or two cases these dogs had been professionally trained and were in all other aspects excellent animals. Yet through bad handling they had reverted to being chasers, and running in.

Let me be absolutely clear about this, you cannot short-circuit this training exercise. It must be so thoroughly implanted in your dog's mind that there is no room for error. If you have followed this book correctly your dog should now respond instantly to the stop whistle. So now comes the crunch, when you will find out if your training has been absolutely thorough.

It is imperative that your dog learns to be 100 per cent reliable and steady with live game, dropping to flush neatly and cleanly. The best way to achieve this is with the help of that old stand-by of the dog trainer, the humble rabbit.

The area you and your dog are going to work on should have light cover, and be devoid of any thickets, brambles, or whins, where your dog can disappear from sight, even for a moment. The ground should hold rabbits, and for the first time do not walk them off. However, a word of caution here. It is most inadvisable to work on ground where the rabbits are currently suffering from myxomatosis, sitting miserably waiting to die. At best they can manage a few blundering, feeble hops, and are guaranteed to invite young dogs to grab them. If your dog does that a few times you can hardly blame him if, when he finds game sitting tight, he dives forward to try and catch it. Naturally, holding a struggling creature will soon teach him to squeeze tighter and kill, and before you know it you have a dog with a hard mouth.

Start working your dog into the wind through light cover, where you will have him in sight at all times. As soon as he indicates that he is on to a bunny blow the stop whistle. Normally, at the sound of the whistle even the most reluctant bunnies will shoot from cover and run away. This is one of the few exercises in training a dog in which you need some luck and good timing. If you blow the stop whistle too soon the dog will drop as he has been trained to, no rabbit will appear, and you will have to carry on until one does. If you take too long before blowing the whistle the dog may well have popped his nose

under the rabbit and started to give chase. Ideally you want to blow your whistle on the instant the rabbit jumps to its feet. If your dog gleefully whizzes after the bolting rabbit blow the stop whistle again, get him back, grab him by the scruff of the neck and take him to the exact spot from where the rabbit came, give him a good shaking, and say 'no, no'.

Be in no doubt about this particular exercise. The dog must not be allowed to chase, and normally a hard shaking, coupled with your raised voice should do the trick. If he persists, however, you must make a stand and chastise him severely. Do not kick him or beat him with a stick. That will get you nowhere and damage the dog. I have found shaking the dog by the scruff of the neck, keeping his feet on the ground, and raging into his face is normally sufficient. It is an enormous temptation to chase a fleeing, bobbing rabbit, and that is why I heavily emphasised making sure that the dog's responses to the stop whistle are perfect earlier in the book.

Try again. Make the dog sit where you put him for, say, half a minute, then cast him out in a different direction and work him on until you come to the next hidden bunny. But make sure you are on the ball. Keep your eye on the dog and the whistle at the ready.

Rabbit pen

Personally I do not think that rabbit pens are necessary for the one man and his dog situation. But if you can justify the expense this is a worthwhile additional aid. The rabbit pen is a captive area where you can keep a rabbit or rabbits in a controlled environment. With this you can steady your dog to flush, particularly if you have no access to ground with a lot of rabbits.

If you are building a permanent rabbit pen, obviously you must make a more robust structure, but for a temporary, short-term pen all you really want to do is beg, borrow or buy a number of posts and chicken wire to construct a pen about 30m square. Make sure the wire is well buried to prevent the rabbits burrowing. Normally burying the wire to a depth of about 20cm should keep the most determined bunnies inside.

The best way to obtain live rabbits for your pen is with ferrets and nets. If you do not keep ferrets yourself there will undoubtedly be someone in your area who does and who would be willing to help you catch a few. It goes without saying of course that you ask the landowner's permission before you go ferreting on his ground.

Pop your rabbits into their pen when you get them home and give them a few days to settle down and become familiar with their surroundings. A dish of fresh water should be available, particularly in the summer, as should supplementary foods if there is not sufficient vegetation to keep them happy.

However, as I have said a number of times before, imagination is the name of the game. If you cannot use a friend's pen, or you feel it is too expensive to make one yourself, then it is possible to use a large pheasant release pen if you can get permission when it is not occupied. But make sure you check right around the perimeter for escape holes since you do not want your precious rabbits disappearing overnight!

In the rabbit pen the procedure is exactly the same as when introducing your dog to rabbits in the wild. But don't over do it. Your dog will quickly become over-familiar with the whole thing, his responses becoming sloppy through boredom. But a dog trained properly up until this stage should present few problems when worked in the open.

Using live birds

There are two other techniques which you can use when teaching your dog to be steady to live game. Go cap in hand to a local pigeon fancier and ask him if you can borrow a couple of his least precious birds. Undertake to pay for them if they are injured in any way. Then with a small spade dig a hole in the ground large enough to hold one of the birds. Get a board made of 15mm (½in) ply which is cut to fit neatly over the hole. Drill a small hole in the wood and attach a length of line to it. Gently put the pigeon into the hole in the ground and lay your board on top. Run the string through the grass. As you work your dog up to where you have hidden the pigeon pick up the string, pull the board off the hole and blow the stop whistle. In this way you can control the release of a bird right under the dog's nose, while at the same time doing away with the uncertainty of knowing when he is likely to flush.

Another widely used technique is that of 'dizzying' a pigeon. Put the pigeon's head under its wing and, holding it gently in both hands, smoothly move it in a circle for about a minute. Then place it in the long grass. Most birds will sit there for up to about ten minutes. Increasing the speed or prolonging the duration of their 'dizzying' will not make them any dizzier or lengthen the time it takes for them to regain their equilibrium, so don't overdo it.

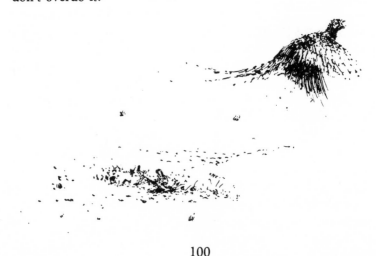

After you have placed the pigeon in the grass get your dog and hunt him up wind toward where you know the bird is crouched. Blow the stop whistle when your dog is just on flushing the bird, and the pigeon will fly off no worse the wear for its experience.

Pointing

For those of you who have decided on a GSP or similar hunting/ pointing breed, the training is exactly the same as for a springer spaniel. Teach the dog to quarter just as I have described, though when you come to quartering range it is better to give a pointer an extra 10m over the spaniel on either side of you. Teach him to drop to flush, to retrieve and all other aspects of the training as laid down. The only difference is in the actual pointing.

Do not be alarmed if your pointer has given no indication of starting to point. Each dog develops this at his own speed, some starting early while others can be well over a year old before this develops. On the other hand, if your dog has reached eighteen months and hasn't yet started, you have cause for concern. But if your dog has been well-bred, don't worry about it, it will come. Once he has given you the slightest indication that he has started to point, you can then begin to refine him.

Take the dog to your training ground, where you have previously walked off the game and hidden a dizzied pigeon. Walk him on a long lead toward where you know the bird is hidden, and as you approach as soon as the dog gives an indication that he has scented the bird he will either take a point and start to creep forward, or point hesitantly. Gently restrain him with the lead, then go forward stroking him gently and run your hand along his back, quietly praising him. Give him a couple of minutes of this (always ready, if the bird happens to spring, to immediately tell him to hup) then gently push him forward with the command 'set'. The instant the game is put up blow your hup whistle, or fire a shot with your starting pistol.

Over the next two or three points feel free to use a long loose lead when working the dog into a hidden bird. You will quickly see when he no longer needs restraint, when he is taking the point easily and happily. Thereafter dispense altogether with the use of a lead, and when the dog takes a point just go forward and gently praise him, keeping him still before giving the command to 'set'. You will find that pointers, once they have learned this new part of their repertoire, will point a wide variety of creatures, from a hedgehog to a rabbit in its burrow. Never briskly call a young dog off a point no matter how silly it appears. Always go up and go through the motions – praise him, gently taking his mind off things by calling him to you and casting him off in another direction.

It may be that your dog will begin to point at an early age, before you have introduced him to flushing game. In that case work him through the whole pointing exercise, polishing up the point, but do not allow him to flush the game at all. Keep him on point and flush the game yourself, making the dog hup of course when the game is flushed. Let him flush only when he is pointing firmly and you reach that stage in his training programme, giving him the command to 'set' as I have already described.

Young dogs, before they have 'experienced noses', have a tendency to point recently vacated positions, where there is a faint scent trace. Don't worry about this for as the dog gets older and more experienced he will soon learn how to differentiate between the smell of an occupied seat and one recently vacated. No matter at what age your dog starts to point ask him only to do so on live game as dead game has a different scent.

Another refinement to a pointing dog, though not entirely necessary, is teaching him to indicate whether he is pointing fur or feather. When you teach your dog to point, and stroke him to make him steady, lift one of his hind legs if he is pointing fur but if feather, lift one of his forelegs. Eventually he will do this without your help.

8

Eighteen months to two years

Your dog should now have completed his apprenticeship, but like most apprentices he will lack experience. Therefore, although he is to all intents and purposes trained, you must at no time allow your control to slip. Even the most experienced dog will at times test your authority. Should you become lax your dog will quickly realise that he can get away with more and more, and pick up the bad habits I have discussed throughout the book. If you have followed each step carefully you should have a well-trained, reliable working gundog. However, it is most important to remember that throughout his working life the occasional refresher course can only do good.

If at any time the dog shows a tendency toward a fault – the most common one being a desire to 'run in' – this should be simple to iron out immediately. Take your dog back to the beginning of a particular task and treat him as a puppy with a quick re-training. This will soon remind him who is master. Of course, as I have already mentioned, if you never allow your dog to anticipate the next command half the potential problems will never arise.

Going shooting for the first time

If all has gone well the dog will now be up to a very high standard, and you will have been through a simulated day's shooting many times, performing each of the actions one might expect in the field, except actually killing game. When you have reached this stage and are 100 per cent certain, with no compromise, it is time to proceed.

I say no compromise, but you must be honest with yourself. Is there any particular aspect of the dog's training that you are not completely satisfied with? If so, resist the temptation to advance. In the long run it is better to wait another few weeks until you are absolutely sure of your dog.

On the first day you intend to take your dog shooting I strongly advise that you ask a friend who is a good shot to assist you. Ask him to leave his own dog at home, irrespective of how good it might be, and go through the motions of a day's shooting, remembering to let your friend know that first and foremost on that day the dog comes first.

Give the dog plenty of time to work his ground while your friend does the shooting. If you can remain on ground which has a good rabbit population, so much the better, but before you go out emphasise to your friend that if he is in any doubt whether the game is dead or not he should shoot it again. The last thing you want on this day are runners.

Each time your friend shoots a rabbit your dog should hup. Leave him sitting while you retrieve most of the close rabbits and those which are lying in full sight, restricting your dog's retrieves to a maximum of one in three. The rabbits your dog retrieves should be ones which he was not able to see lying, and give yourself time to work him on to them.

Unless your friend is an exceptionally good shot, it is unwise for you to go after pheasants on this first day since these birds, particularly if they are strong runners, can travel quite fantastic distances before they couch, and it is not a good idea to ask a young dog on his first day out to take a line which may cross several fields.

It is also important that you do not allow a young dog to go after a runner until the wounded creature has disappeared from sight and crouched in cover. It is really asking too much to expect the dog to know the difference between a fleeing hare which he has put up, and one carrying shot which has been wounded. To the dog they both represent one thing, a chase, and at this stage that must be avoided at all costs.

After you have worked your dog on one or two days with the aid of a shooting friend you can try taking him out on your own, doing the shooting yourself. However, remain aware that at this

105

stage the dog must come first. Do not get carried away, thinking you can relax. The dog may be well trained, but like the graduate of a medical school who is still a long way from performing brain surgery, your young dog must be given time and attention to gain experience, and you must be there at all times to help him resist temptations.

If your friend and shooting companion is a dog owner you must be realistic about the quality of both his training and handling of his animal. Nothing ruins a dog quicker than seeing an older dog committing crimes, and the guaranteed way to cow your dog is to let him witness another dog getting a beating in the field. So if your chum leaves anything to be desired as a handler, my sincere advice to you is to tell him the truth – either he leaves his dog at home, or you won't take yours. Better still, go on your own.

Whatever you do avoid taking a young dog into the field accompanied by another dog which is not properly trained. I remember a classic example of this. A fellow went out with his young dog and an older more experienced dog. When a hare got up the fellow shot and missed and the old dog set off in pursuit. The owner, when he finally managed to call the older dog back, set about giving it a beating. When he turned around the young dog was standing about 100m away wondering what was what. The fellow had just placed the idea firmly into the dog's head that a combination of a hare and firing a shot resulted in a beating. For the rest of its life that dog never quite got over this early lesson.

On the brighter side, if you are fortunate enough to have a friend with a good working dog that is free of vices, then an excellent idea is for both of you to work your dogs. The animals will quickly become used to this, both of them of course dropping to flush and shot. Send them out to retrieve each other's game. This is a superb way of impressing and consolidating discipline in the field, when one dog has to remain on hup while another trots past him to retrieve. In this way both dogs will gain, irrespective of age.

One last word on this subject. If your dog is ever in a situation where he is going out to pick up a retrieve and you see another dog rushing toward him, halt your dog on the stop whistle and call him back to you. Do not allow him to get involved in a tug of war with game. The dog with such a display of bad manners is purely emphasising both his own and his master's lack of control, and such occasions and individuals should be avoided at all costs.

Picking up

Picking up is the best way I know to give you not only excellent opportunities to work your dog and improve and polish your handling of him, but as an added bonus you also get the opportunity to meet shoot owners and keepers. If both you and your dog behave yourselves, and you do not thrust yourself upon your hosts such occasions can result in an invitation to a cock shoot or two. Once you have established a rapport with the headkeeper your chances of getting pigeon and rabbit shooting increase greatly.

Depending on the area you live in, you can find that the local estate has many people willing to pick up or, on the other hand as is often the case, there is a shortage of willing bodies with good dogs. When you first approach the keeper keep in mind that he is doing you a favour, and it is not the other way around. Too often people assume familiarity with keepers. Remember the man has probably worked all year, producing birds to put over the guns for a few days in the winter, and he is certainly not going to want anyone to jeopardise his day by getting in the way and making a mess of things. So ask him nicely, telling him the truth about your dog's standard and experience.

If the first thing the keeper offers you is either beating or picking up for walking guns driving toward a standing line, I would not accept. Tell him that until your dog is much more experienced you would rather not have it exposed to a walking line, with other dogs, moving people, and many firing guns.

The real reason I do not recommend you beat or go with the walking guns is slightly different. I have seen some real clowns with the most fiendish brutes, going under the disguise of dogs and handlers, in line. With the general commotion, barrage of shots, whistles blowing, dogs moving about, falling birds, runners, and so on, it is really asking a little too much of both you and your dog, and tempting fate unnecessarily. Instead, ask the keeper if you can pick up for a standing gun. If he agrees, first introduce yourself to the gun at your stand. Then position yourself about 40m straight behind him, making sure that he knows where you are. Do not attach yourself to a gun who has brought his own dog, unless he is going to keep it on the lead.

When the drive starts stay still and watch the sport. It is not a bad idea to take a pad and paper with you. Draw a little circle representing the gun and another representing your own position. Each time a bird is down mark the position on the paper with a small X. This will help you to remember, particularly if you are inexperienced, where birds have fallen.

To make sure that you get things right I always recommend that you ask the keeper how he wants you to handle the retrieves. Does he want them picked up immediately or left until after the drive. In the case of strong runners, that is birds obviously winged, most keepers will suggest the dog is put away pretty quickly. However, at this stage in the proceedings it is normally left to your own assessment of the situation.

If you see a bird, obviously hit, planing on some distance behind you before gliding down, the chances are that it is a strong runner. If the bird has gone straight into the next covert do not send your dog charging through it. It is really up to you to use your intuition.

Once again, when you are picking up, work your dog carefully and watch for other dogs. If it is obvious that another dog is after the same bird stop your dog with the whistle, and call him in. This is not only observing etiquette, but is plain good sense.

Remember always at the end of the day to thank the keeper for having you.

Advanced water retrieving

If you intend shooting ducks or geese it is very important that you give your dog regular water work in the darkness. However, I have kept this section to a late stage in training so that the dog is confident and steady when working out of your sight.

Your dog is at a great disadvantage when working in water. Although by now he will be retrieving confidently from water such work will have been done during daylight, a very different kettle of fish from what you will expect him to do at dawn or dusk, which are the normal flighting times for ducks and geese. Then the dog must be able to work out of your sight, using his initiative and the experience which you have carefully provided. So it is now, when the dog is completely capable and confident in every aspect of working on land, that you should start the introduction to darkness.

Take the dog to the pond or river where you normally work, in the dusk before it is too dark, and work him on a mixture of previously hidden retrieves and thrown decoys both in the water

and onto the far bank. Over subsequent visits work in progressively darker conditions, with the eventual aim of being able to put the dog out in total darkness, with only the aid of a distant splash as your decoy hits the water to indicate direction.

You will find in running water that most dogs quickly learn the trick of running downstream before entering, so that they can swim straight out to the approaching decoy. This is not a skill that you can easily teach them. It is learnt only through the dog's own experience. He will learn that when a bird falls downstream he will get to it quicker by running down the bank and going in below it to intercept. I never cease to marvel, when watching my own dog, which has developed this skill to a very high degree, at how he manages to relate the speed of the current to where it is necessary to enter the water, yet he does so every time with unfailing accuracy. Many times I could have taken bets that my dog was going too far downstream, but he always succeeds.

It has been my experience that most dogs which work regularly on rivers soon develop this particular skill. It is, however, possible to help an inexperienced young dog to acquire this facility. If you are working by a river stop the dog opposite you on the far bank and send him further up the bank, putting him at hup when he is say 20m upstream of you. Then call him to you.

With any luck he will enter the water and the current will carry him straight toward you. If on the other hand he runs downstream back to the point nearest you before entering the water, there is not much you can do about it, and certainly do not press the dog for, as I have said, this particular skill is one which really cannot be taught and is learned naturally through experience.

When you are working your dog in water it is well to remember that if he gets tired while working on land he can always pace himself, or even stop for a rest, but in water there is no chance to relax or stop, so never, never overtire a dog in this element or in any way risk that extra swim.

Wildfowling

One area where so many otherwise well-trained gundogs and handlers seem to get into difficulties is in shooting ducks and geese. Far too often I have met people who start to apologise for their dog before we reach the water, making the excuse that the animal is not used to carrying heavy geese and pointing out that there is a vast difference between working a dog on decoys in a pond and putting him through icy water in the darkness.

Let us imagine that you are sitting at a goose flighting pond in the gathering dusk. Some geese come over and you shoot one which falls far out in the water. Then as your dog is on the point of grabbing the goose, which has been wounded, the bird dives out of sight to reappear again some 30m further on, and your dog churns after it. Then as the dog approaches the goose again, hey presto, Mr Goose disappears. What should you do? If you allow the dog to swim continuously around in circles you will quickly sap his energy, and he will be so keen to collect the bird that he will be completely unaware of the return journey to be made to the shore. In such circumstances it is imperative that you call your dog off, and he must obey you. Yet so often in the heat of the moment people have real difficulty calling their dog back to land without the bird, which the dog may see only a few yards in front of him, and this is due entirely to a lack of training in water.

Another problem underlying the need for quiet, quick and total control can arise when you have two geese down, a right and a left, one close by, the other some distance away. One bird has skimmed on before falling and is clearly going to be a very strong runner. You must obviously be able to direct your dog with a minimum of arm waving and whistle blowing for the second bird since speed and silence under such circumstances are absolutely necessary if you do not wish to spoil any subsequent shooting that evening for yourself or your companions.

It is difficult to believe that a large wounded goose can be such an incredible escape artist, being able to cover long distances quickly before tucking itself into the most surprising spots, and it is very important that when you put your dog out, possibly in almost total darkness to where you cannot see him working, that you give him time to work the ground and find the bird. Your dog may be away from you for some time and only experience will tell you when he has had long enough and you should call him back.

Never, never allow your dog onto ice. Ignore the clown who will tell you that his dog is fearless and will force his way through thin ice to pick up a fallen bird. Unless you are fully prepared to go in to the rescue in the event of the dog going through the ice do not take the chance. You could be sending him to his death.

9
Field trials

The majority of shooting men do not bother entering their dogs for field trials or field tests simply because they are not really interested in such events. As I mentioned at the beginning, dog owners generally fall into two basic categories – dog men and shooting men, and it is usually the former that go in for trialing. However, if you are interested in having a go, do not be intimidated by the reputations and standing of either the canine or human competitors.

Much has been written in both books and magazines giving novices advice on the best method to start trialing, but it is my belief that it is one subject in which, irrespective of how much print you read, there is no substitute for practical experience. So before you start to take your dog along to these events go to several purely as a spectator. Study the scene, the general requirements and standards. You will meet other handlers who should be pleased to offer advice and assistance to any newcomer. The trialing fraternity, like any other body, has its personalities, jealousies, favourites, and gossip-mongers. But in the main the majority of people I have met in the trialing world are only too keen to assist and advise new recruits to their circle.

You should join the field trial society of your dog's particular breed fairly early on in the animal's career, preferably when he is about nine months old and is hinting at future potential. This will mean that you stand a much better chance of being drawn for a place in trials, as all too often there are more dogs entered than can possibly be run, and new members to the society unfortunately have to wait until more established members have been drawn. Remember too that if you wish to enter your dog in a field trial he must be registered with the Kennel Club. This can take some time to process so again, do it early.

Once you have made the decision to enter your dog it is as well for you to sharpen him up. Like any athlete about to be put through a test, it is as well to prepare your dog for each event, giving him an increase in high protein foods, meats and supplements. Two excellent foods to give your dog at this time are raw liver and tripe. Both are inexpensive and very nutritious. At the same time step up exercise until the dog achieves peak fitness.

Your visits to trials will have shown you the form of such days and the best plan therefore while you prepare your dog for one is to organise several days' shooting during which you can try to simulate trial procedure.

Spaniel trials

If you are fortunate enough to have a friend with a good dog who can work with you then that is considerably more desirable and is a marvellous way of getting your dog used to working with other dogs and handlers. Obviously you should use ground that has a fair population of game to give your dog something to work with.

Let both dogs hunt across their 'patches' together, in their normal stylish fashion, and if your own dog is the first to find and flush game keep him in the drop position, shoot the bird or rabbit, and let your friend's dog perform the retrieve. Then when the other dog flushes game your dog should retrieve it to you, and so on . . . as many variations as you can come up with, since the judges in a trial will be watching for fidgets and lack of self-discipline. All the effort you put in beforehand in this area will certainly show up on the day.

114

It is also very important that you get your dog (and yourself) used to working while other dogs, handlers, and spectators are there. So if Great Aunt Maude and her fifty-two nephews and nieces want to come along and watch you putting your dog through his paces, by all means welcome them if it will help you and the dog get over the nervous jitters of the 'first-time' performer. Equally important is that your dog should be content to sit in a mannerly fashion while other dogs are performing.

Great speed should not be a major factor among your dog's accomplishments, but a plodder is also not desirable, so if your dog has a tendency to be a bit on the slow side try giving him less food, and less exercise before a training period, or take him out early in the morning when he will tend to be fresher. The actual time you will be 'on stage' during a trial will be fairly short, perhaps fifteen to thirty minutes, so it is a good idea to get your dog used to performing over such an interval, and then stopping.

Use your whistle judiciously and only when essential. Always refrain from speaking to your dog. Although not a serious crime, speaking to your dog during a trial when you could just as easily use your whistle can cost you valuable points.

You should start your sharpening-up exercises as much as five to six weeks before the trial takes place. Attune responses, go through the training schedule methodically and if you encounter a problem ascertain why it has occurred and then put it right. There's no point in thinking it will be all right on the day and hoping for the best. That will only serve to waste your time, and the judges' too for that matter.

It is vital that your dog stops sharply when flushing game. Use your stop whistle for this. When the dog is working ground he must search every little nook and cranny, anywhere game may be lurking. Give him blind retrieves, he may get a runner during the trial, so try and practise taking a line, and give him water retrieves too. However, a word of caution here. Although your dog is a finely tuned, well-educated animal he can still get bored or over-confident with retrieving, and even now you should do at least half the retrieving yourself. This will also serve to practise the dog's self-control and steadiness.

Serious faults during a trial will cause your dog to be eliminated from the entire procedure. Such failings include barking or making any sort of noise, running in, chasing, hard-mouth, missing game when hunting, or failing to give up the catch when told to. Other faults which will count against you, though may not necessarily disqualify you are general lack of control, noisy handling, careless and untidy work, unsteadiness or changing birds. A general rule of thumb is that your dog should do everything that he would usually do on a normal day's shooting correctly and with style. This is what the judges have in mind when assessing the performances.

The trial
While you are inexperienced your first few forays will be in novice trials. All dogs entering such trials are beginners and the judges will generally speaking be more tolerant and give a little more leeway during a run. This is not to say that you should skimp on your dog's training. It is better to have a dog that is a cut above the rest than a mediocre member of the pack.

If the trial you are entering is a long way away it is as well to travel to the event on the day before so that you, and more importantly your dog, are fresh and not suffering from the after-effects of a long car journey. Give your dog a nourishing light breakfast on the day of the trial, and a fifteen-minute exercise period. Then relax. It should not be necessary to have a little extra workout if you have done your preparatory work together. Be cool, try to avoid 'first night' nerves. It is after all no big deal, though some trialing enthusiasts appear to regard it as such. If you start to get anxious and nervous, as sure as eggs is eggs you will transfer that to your dog, with the obvious results.

When you arrive at the venue keep your dog on the lead, find the Secretary and introduce yourself, telling him what number you have been drawn. Unless yours is one of the first two dogs, join the spectators and watch the action. Whatever you do, try to keep calm. Remember that there is always a degree of luck in trials since no two retrieves are the same. One retrieve can be short and simple, while the next is a veritable marathon.

Retrieving a heavy greylag goose over a high wall

A good delivery of a
greylag goose

A nicely retrieved
partridge

Mallard, partridge and pigeon in the trailer—a successful day's shooting

After the morning flight

A good bag of partridge

There are two judges in spaniel trials, each of whom takes a dog, so that there are always two dogs working at one time. When it is nearing your turn the steward will signal you to come forward, which you should do, but remain behind the judge until you are actually told by him to move up into the line, at which time you will remove the lead from your dog and your trial will begin.

Your dog will be required to hunt in front of the two guns who will be positioned on either side of you. Hunt your dog carefully and methodically, as if you were on sparsely populated ground, to the very edges of his patch. When your dog flushes use the stop whistle. You may be told to retrieve the game, or you may not. Never anticipate the judge's wishes. If you hear a shot going off at the other end of the line, drop your dog immediately with your whistle. If you have not yet had a retrieve, or the other judge, for whatever reason, does not want his dog to have it, you may be asked to take the retrieve in his place. Although you are not compelled to accept, you ought to, so make absolutely certain that you get precise direction as to where the game lies before putting your dog out. It is one thing giving your dog a blind retrieve, but quite another having a blind one yourself.

When the judge indicates to you that he is satisfied with your first run put your dog on the lead and return to the body of spectators. Play modest and watch the proceedings until you are called forward again to run under the second judge. If there have been eliminations in the first run you may be called forward quite quickly, so stay on call. Your turn under the second judge should be similar to the first.

If you have not been eliminated from the trial you should be satisfied with that, particularly on your first few outings. As I said previously luck always plays its part in field trials and you should be neither too down-hearted if you are eliminated nor too big-headed if you are placed among the winners. Next time it could go the other way.

When the trial is over the judges will compare notes to see if they are in agreement as to the winning dogs. Often, if their opinions do not concur they will ask the top few dogs to run-off.

During a run-off the dogs, normally three or four, will perform simultaneously, giving the judges another opportunity to compare the style, ability, and general work.

When it is all over the certificates will be handed out and congratulations offered. You can go home with your young dog, content in the knowledge that you both have been initiated and have come through the experience unscathed. You will be ready to try again another time, when Lady Luck might well be on your side.

Retriever trials

Retriever trials are entirely different from spaniel trials in that your dog will not be expected to hunt, but to walk confidently at heel until told to retrieve, a task he should carry out flawlessly.

The preparation of labrador retrievers for a trial should be similar to that for spaniels, but without the hunting/flushing exercise. In fact, as I said in the introduction to this book, if you intend putting your labrador into field trials it is not a good idea to let him hunt at all, since at a field trial your dog will have to perform long, straight retrieves. If he has been taught to hunt, his natural instinct will be to do so, and he will be less inclined to go far out from you on a long, unmarked retrieve.

As in spaniel trials the labrador in a retriever trial will be expected to perform in front of an audience, and with other dogs

retrieving. So once more the ideal situation is to go shooting with a friend and his well trained dog. On the other hand, if your shooting friend's dog does not come up to scratch, best leave it be and sharpen up your dog alone. As I have said in previous chapters dogs can easily pick up bad habits from each other, and the last thing you want when you are preparing your dog for a field trial is for him to start imitating the bad behaviour of another dog.

Do at least half the retrieves yourself. Your dog must never get the idea that he has a right to every retrieve. This will tend to make him more positive in sitting, listening, and waiting patiently for your signal to fetch.

Style, natural ability at marking, taking direction, and retrieving neatly to hand are what count in retriever trials, so concentrate on the quality of your dog's work, polishing up where necessary. Work your dog as silently as you can, since noisy handling will cost valuable points and should be completely unnecessary. Practise your directional commands, particularly the 'go back' signal as chances are that you will be given a very long, unmarked retrieve and your dog should be able to go far out after it. Confidence and style are required, and if you bear in mind that all you are doing is going through what happens on a normal shooting day in the space of fifteen minutes or so, and observing the correct etiquette, then you cannot go far wrong.

A retriever trial, like a spaniel trial, is really a form of elimination contest, with dogs gaining or dropping points in a series of natural shooting tasks that they could reasonably be expected to perform in the field, with the emphasis on the standard of both the dog's work and how he responds to his handler. The judges' job is seldom easy. They will eliminate a dog for running in, refusing to enter water, barking or giving tongue, being hardmouthed, or being out of control, and regard noisy handling, poor control, unsteadiness, changing birds and sloppy work as serious faults. You should seek to score points on marking ability, speed, style in both finding game and retrieving, general style, carriage, flair and control.

Now while I say a hard mouth is a serious crime, in the event of your dog bringing a damaged bird to you during a trial do not try to hide the damage when you hand the bird to the judge, or try to put one over on him. This rarely succeeds, and the judge will be less than pleased at your attempt to cover-up. Remember that birds can be damaged on falling, and if you know that your dog is not hard-mouthed, yet has retrieved a torn bird, point this out to the judge, and he will respect you the more, though he will certainly watch the dog quite intently on his next run, and examine the retrieve carefully. It is also as well to bear in mind that although your dog will be penalised if he drops a bird on the retrieve, he will not be marked down if he lays the bird down after the initial pick up in order to improve his grip.

It is a fact, though a sad one in my opinion, that a speedy dog which can dash out after his game, pick it up quickly, and tally-ho back to his handler, will usually beat the slow, methodical worker which prefers to take his time and use his own senses rather than rely heavily on the visual or whistle commands of his handler.

As I said at the beginning of this book, it seems almost as though a third strain of labrador has been developed, purely for trialing – the small, slim dog which bears little resemblance to the original labrador retriever, and yet such animals are winning many of the top field trials. When I commented on the slimness of a labrador bitch belonging to a friend of mine, a member of the Northern Ireland gundog team, he agreed that she was exceedingly slim – 'thin as a tick . . . she's a fast one, and she'll catch the eyes of the judges all right.'

However, having said that, do not be discouraged if your young dog is not a fast worker. He may turn out to be of a very high standard overall and his lack of speed may not prejudice his chances in field trials. Try him at a few field tests before going on to novice trials and see how he compares with the rest of the field. A field test is simply that – a test of basic abilities using dummies; the dogs are all given set retrieves, no unmarked retrieves, no runners, and each dog performs on its own.

Novice trials, and open trials or stakes are entirely different mattters. They are both proper trials, with all the hazards and unreliability involved with shooting live game. Naturally you would not think of entering your inexperienced dog into an open stake, whereas novice trials are more relaxed affairs and their judges are generally not as strict on the young dogs as they would be in an open event.

The trial

In retriever trials there are either three or four judges in the line. If there are three judges each will have two dogs under his immediate eye; therefore six dogs work at one time. If four judges are taking part they work in pairs and only four dogs are in the line together.

Having travelled to the venue on the previous night, give your dog a light breakfast and a ten minute exercise period. Don't try 'cramming' him on the morning of the trial; it will do no good whatsoever. If your dog is going to be on the ball on the day he will not need the refresher course, and if he is to have an off day, another ten minutes, or even half an hour is going to do no good at all; it may make him more agitated and nervous. You may even make yourself feel worse and this depression can transfer to your dog. So the vicious circle begins. Therefore be calm, take it all in your stride and hope for the best.

Once you have introduced yourself to the field trial secretary, and given him the number you have drawn, you can join the spectators behind the line of judges, guns, and competitors. If you are drawn in the first six you will probably be called up first. In this case you will take your dog on the lead and report to your judge, who will tell you where to stand. Don't anticipate the judge's commands, and do nothing until he tells you to, even leaving your lead on the dog until you are told to take it off. With all the excitement your dog may suddenly decide to bolt after a fleeing rabbit and your trialing day may be abruptly terminated!

As the line moves forward and game gets up and is shot, the dogs are given the retrieves. It is entirely at the judge's discretion which dog is given each retrieve, so do not assume that since your dog is nearest to a bird he will be asked to retrieve it. It may be that you have already had one or two easy retrieves and your judge wishes to give someone from the other end of the line a chance at a fairly difficult, unmarked retrieve. If this is the case your dog will be expected to sit at heel quietly and at ease, watching as another dog is worked right out in front of all the dogs, handlers, judges, and guns.

If you are asked to take a retrieve that you have not seen, from the other end of the line, be sure you know the precise direction where the bird has fallen. It is also important that you know the wind direction so that you can direct your dog downwind of fallen game. The judge will tell you when he has finished with you and you can then join the following spectators.

You will be under another judge during the second run of a trial, and the procedure should be the same. However, if there is a drive your dog must be able to sit quietly and peacefully with birds falling all around, without becoming so excited that he runs in after a winged cock pheasant. Elimination would follow.

As I said previously, when dealing with spaniel trials, luck plays a great part when you combine the imponderables of live game, weather and uneven ground. It is also worthwhile remembering that your dog is being judged only on his performance over one day. The judge does not know that yesterday your dog performed a distant unmarked retrieve beautifully, but today he just cannot seem to find the game at all. The judge is required to assess the dog on his work only at that trial. This is entirely correct, though bad luck if your dog is off form. Conversely, your dog may not have had the opportunity to shine because of an abundance of easy retrieves, and the dog which happens to get a few difficult retrieves and manages to pull them off with confidence will win on this occasion.

So if your first excursion into the trialing world is less than propitious don't be discouraged from having another go, you'll soon get hooked on it and will discover a rewarding hobby.

Trialing with hunting, pointing and retrieving dogs

If you are the owner of one of those all-round gundogs which hunt, point and retrieve, and you wish to enter it into field trials, read the section dealing with spaniels to give you the general idea of what will be expected of you and your dog. Field trials with these all-rounders are run by the various breed societies. GSP, vizsla and weimaraner all take similar form. Since these dogs hunt, the trial is conducted in the same manner as in spaniel trials, and your dog should be given the same pre-trial sharpening up exercises.

A dog will be run singly under the eye of two judges with two or three guns along the line beside the judge and handler. As with spaniels these dogs are required to quarter their ground efficiently and confidently and to point steadily until the guns are ready to shoot. They should flush on command and wait until told to retrieve. If the flushed game is not shot the dog should carry on with his quartering as before.

They will also be asked to do at least one water retrieve. The dogs are usually walked over different types of ground, to show their full range of abilities. It may be that the morning outing will be through light woodland or similar area, and the afternoon run will take place over moorland or open fields, showing the dogs' versatility in working conditions.

With these trials, as in trialing with any breed of dog, the whole idea is to simulate a normal day's shooting, with the dogs showing off their abilities under similar conditions, and of course major faults will cause your dog to be eliminated from the trial. These include barking, hard-mouth, running in, chasing game, and so on. You the handler must also refrain from noisy handling and show that you know what you are doing.

If you have a dog that performs to trialing standard and you enjoy the atmosphere, the excitement, and the friendships made in the trialing circle, then by all means have a go at it. But be honest with yourself; if your dog, after a few encounters, does not seem to have what it takes, don't waste your time and money by continuing to enter him in novice stakes hoping that everything will go perfectly for once. You must either accept that you will have to confine your activities with your dog to solo outings, or try again with another dog which may prove to have that little extra something that makes a field trial champion.

10

Bitches and breeding

For those of you with bitches a little understanding of their anatomy should be of value.

Seasons

Probably the greatest handicap in owning a bitch is that she can come into heat in the middle of the shooting season. This can be very inconvenient, particularly if you are to shoot with a companion with a male dog, since the smell of the bitch will thoroughly distract that other dog. My advice on such occasions is to leave your bitch at home.

There are a number of preparations which you can spray around the hindquarters of the bitch to help mask the smell and thus lessen the interest of other dogs, but they are not 100 per cent effective and the only sensible action for you to take when your bitch is in season and you do not wish her to have pups, is to keep her away from dogs for a while. Also, a bitch which has been served in the past invariably has enjoyed the experience and thus heightened natural instincts. Consequently her interests are often more directed to going off and finding a convenient male dog rather than the tasks you have in mind.

Usually a bitch will come into season every six months, that season lasting on average twenty-one days. The event is easily noticed and you should get plenty of warning. The vulva will swell and leak drops of blood. Some bitches are quite diligent about keeping themselves clean and will seem to be continuously licking themselves, but others are less so.

After about ten days the colour of the fluid will change, becoming clearer, but will continue seeping until the end of the period in season. If you intend to mate the bitch it is at the time the colour change takes place that conception is most likely.

False pregnancy

This condition occurs more often than is generally realised, though some animals seem much more prone to this than others. A friend of mine had a dog which was a maiden bitch, yet throughout her life she continuously developed false pregnancies. The dog's owner was not particularly diligent in keeping her away from heat and fluids, allowing her to lie beside the gas fire until her hair singed, and giving her unlimited water. The dog continued the false pregnancy through to the point where milk actually dribbled freely from the teats. To those who have never seen this condition it really can be quite mystifying.

Usually bitches which are going to have a false pregnancy will develop all the signs of a normal pregnancy around six to nine weeks after they have been in season, starting with a slight swelling of the abdomen. The bitch becomes quite 'broody' and to all intents and purposes you could easily be excused for assuming she has become pregnant.

Eventually the bitch can reach the stage of preparing a nest for expected arrival of the litter, which of course never comes. They often take possession of some household item such as a child's teddy bear or even an old sock, directing all their maternal instincts towards it, carrying it about and defending it for all the world as though it was a defenceless pup.

If your dog develops such a condition the best method of treatment is to take her to your vet who will prescribe a course of tablets to clear it up. You must make the effort to give the bitch lots of exercise, keep her away from heat, and restrict liquid intake. You must not just allow events to take their course. You can cause your bitch a great deal of confusion and mental unrest, so act promptly if this condition develops.

Spaying

Spaying is probably an unnecessary subject to include in a book on gundogs since few people who have gone to the trouble of buying a bitch would be likely to do away with the possibility of breeding in future years. However, some people do prefer the character of a bitch with no intention of breeding from her, and the inconvenience of the animal coming into season regularly can be avoided by spaying.

There is a commonly held belief that animals which have been spayed tend to put on weight, becoming fat and lethargic. This is not true. A bitch which has been spayed requires less food than her fertile sisters since her mental state is more serene. So therefore a spayed bitch must have her diet cut down to avoid any weight gain.

The operation itself is a relatively simple one for your vet to perform and it is arguable that it has certain advantages in that the bitch will no longer be prone to any form of gynaecological problems in later years, and obviously will not have false pregnancies. I will not go into the argument of whether or not it is 'right' to do this. It is entirely a personal decision of the dog owner who must weigh the advantages against the disadvantages to suit his personal needs. The only other advice I would give on this particular subject is that you should make the decision while the bitch is still young, ideally three to four months old. Discuss it with your vet who will advise you when is the best time to carry out the operation.

Regarding castration, there is really no reason why this should ever be done unless your dog is an habitual fighter or is continually running away. In either case he would be useless as a gundog anyway, and I would advise that rather than even consider this course of action you sell the dog.

Mating

If you have a dog which you do not intend to use as a stud dog and a friend asks you for a service it is well to understand the implications your co-operation can have. Dogs which have been used for stud purposes have their natural desires and instincts greatly enhanced, and you should remember this as once they have tasted the delights of a willing bitch they will be prone to pursue bitches with greater enthusiasm.

One of the most natural instincts of any dog owner who is fond of his animal is to try and perpetuate the line, to breed with the dog so that you can use the offspring. However, before you do anything you must be honest with yourself and in your heart of hearts ask yourself if the dog is good enough. Does it have faults, either physically or in its abilities? If you are not absolutely satisfied with your own answers don't go any further and be happy with what you have. You are doing no one any favours by perpetuating a less than ideal strain.

So, having decided that your bitch is good enough and you want to breed a litter of puppies from her, plan the event well in advance so that you are certain as to which dog is going to be used for the 'service'. If you are intending to take your bitch to a stud dog then you would certainly be well advised to telephone the breeder and book the service well in advance, giving the owner of the dog an indication of the time your bitch is likely to be in season. A professional stud dog owner would normally insist on having sight of your dog's pedigree and would tell you if the mating was not advisable on the grounds of common ancestry. If on the other hand you are using the services of a friend's or a local dog examine the pedigrees of both animals scrupulously. Avoid mating of dogs with common heritage, and at all costs if this is any closer than great-grandparents. Ideally two entirely separate lines should be sought.

If you take your bitch to a professional stud dog you will be expected to pay a fee which I advise you to check on in advance. If on the other hand you are using an amateur it is accepted practice that the stud dog owner has the pick of the litter. If you do not wish to enter into this arrangement then discuss payment with the dog owner as compensation for a pup. Whatever you do make quite sure you have cleared up the 'business' arrangements before the deed is done.

Do not be tempted to take a litter from your bitch until, at the earliest, her training is fully completed and, if you plan your calendar right, having the pups in the early spring, the bitch will certainly be well back in trim before the start of the following shooting season.

131

When your dog starts to come into season you have ten to twelve days to wait before the colour and consistency of her discharge changes and fertility is at a peak. Immediately the season starts, notify the stud dog owner, giving him advance warning. It is normal practice for the bitch to be taken to the dog but you should try to avoid long car journeys immediately prior to the hoped-for service. If you have booked the services of a professional dog some distance away travel with the bitch on the day prior to the event. With the professional dog take the advice of the breeder who will inform you as to procedure.

Whatever you do, do not expect to stand over your dog. Normally problems only arise when two inexperienced dog owners decide to put their dogs together to mate. Their enthusiasm and desire to get things right often only leads to problems. Probably the worst example of this I have ever encountered was some years ago when a fellow I knew only as a passing acquaintance asked me for a service from my GSP dog, Rommel. His bitch was four and a half years old and had been to several dogs, always without success. I was confident that Rommel could perform the task since it's a job which he is particularly keen on, so I told the chap to come on the appointed date.

I assure you that it is no exaggeration when I tell you that when the day came the man arrived with his wife, four children, two friends and their family who were staying with them, in two car-loads. God only knows what they expected or what their ideas were, but the bitch was bouncing about like a rubber ball, and when I put her in the enclosure with Rommel she was only interested in getting back to the line of grinning faces. I insisted they all left and take a walk with me. Full of suspicion the fellow started asking me how he would know if the service had been performed. I told him to keep calm and to wait and see.

Anyway we walked about 100m away and stood chatting. After ten minutes or so I heard the bitch give a yelp and told the man that he alone should return with me to the enclosure to see the 'evidence'. The moral of that story is quite simple. This foolish man and his family were obviously transferring their anxiety/interest to the bitch.

Incidentally that particular story has a postscript which may serve as a word of warning to anyone thinking of allowing his dog to be used for stud. In his anxiety to hold the bitch down Rommel caught the loose skin in the back of her neck with his teeth and made a few tiny punctures. The idiot owner actually thought he could sue me for damages!

When you take your bitch to a dog put them together in some form of enclosure, and unless both dogs are obviously keen to start proceedings get out of sight and watch them from a hidden spot. What usually happens is that the bitch frisks about with the dog which gets progressively more excited, standing stiff-legged with tail erect, then bounces after her licking her hindquarters. The bitch will 'stand' when she is ready, pushing her hind-quarters out with her tail held up and to one side.

After the dog has mounted, something called 'tying' takes place, which might alarm the inexperienced. The dog's penis appears to be stuck inside the bitch and they finish up standing end to end. This can last from five minutes to an hour and is entirely natural and normal. Under no circumstances must you in any way attempt to separate them. If either dog becomes agitated, and it would probably be the bitch, it is permissible for the owner to soothe his dog by stroking it and preventing it from pulling. Eventually they will free themselves and that is that.

The likelihood of conception is greatly increased if another service is performed the next day. When the dog has pulled free from the bitch the inexperienced are often surprised and alarmed at what seems like a very large, semi-erect, bright red, swollen penis that has not retracted. Again this is entirely normal and no attempt should be made to assist the dog.

When you put the dogs together if you discover that the bitch is bouncing all over the place with the dog getting over-excited it can end up with the dog making several unsuccessful attempts to mount the bitch until he is exhausted and has ejaculated most of his sperm. In this case you will have to try another day.

Other problems are that the bitch will either snarl and snap at the dog or sit down and growl. In these circumstances usually your timing is wrong so don't proceed any further. A young male dog which has never serviced a bitch before can get quite a shock when the object of his desires starts to snarl at him, but you will find in nine times out of ten that by keeping the dogs calm and relaxed and by putting them together in a natural way nature will eventually take its course.

Very occasionally a young male dog acting on instinct alone will mount a willing bitch which is standing, but he doesn't know quite what to do, pushing forward without actually entering the bitch. In such cases it is permissible for the dog owner to neatly take the erect penis between thumb and forefinger when the dog has mounted the bitch and just guide it in. Be assured, I have never met a dog that needed such direction more than once.

Bitches in whelp

At first there is little sign that your bitch has conceived, though within the first three weeks the embryos will fully develop. Then during the next six weeks they grow and develop in the womb. The pups will be carried for nine weeks (sixty-three days), but you should not be alarmed if the delivery is two or three days late or early. The bitch will begin to swell and the mammary glands will enlarge. Your correct treatment of the bitch during pregnancy is vital.

During the first half of the pregnancy you should increase the bitch's food, and during the second half increase it yet again. However, when I say increase the food I do not mean that you should provide an enormous pile to eat but rather increase the number of feed times. This will prevent the bitch becoming bloated and uncomfortable. Quality and quantity control now will secure the welfare of the growing, unborn puppies as well as maintain the bitch's general health. Do not increase carbohydrates – meal, biscuits, etc, but step up meat and proteins, allowing as much milk as required, and get mineral supplements from your vet.

Also during the pregnancy keep the bitch well exercised, though during the latter stages do not expect galloping about. A fat, lethargic bitch is more likely to encounter a difficult pregnancy than a fit, active, healthy one is.

It is important that you watch the condition of the bitch. If her back starts to broaden too much you are over-feeding, and for goodness sake do not let any well-meaning amateur squeeze her stomach in an attempt to tell you how far on she is. That is a job for the experienced, and your vet can do it without danger.

Before the puppies are born prepare the place of delivery. If the bitch is kept in the house a large cardboard box well lined with thick, warm bedding and covered in layers of newspapers will suffice. The sides of the cardboard box should be high enough to prevent the young puppies from waddling out. It should be warm and draught-free. Encourage the bitch to use it as a bed, making it as comfortable as possible. If whelping is to be in a kennel it is a good idea to suspend an infra-red lamp not less than a metre above the nest.

Normally when a bitch is about to whelp she goes off her food for about twenty-four hours beforehand. During the last few days of pregnancy you will notice a difference in the bitch's behaviour as she scratches the bedding, continuously trying to make it more comfortable. It is at this point that you should put in some nesting materials. Newspapers are ideal, for the bitch can tear and distribute them. When whelping begins it is advisable to be on hand, and as a precaution telephone your vet to check on where he will be in the event that you need him. But do not try to help unless the bitch is getting into difficulties.

The bitch's stomach will start to contract on pushing for delivery. These muscle contractions and period of straining will be punctuated by periods of rest and will become more frequent just before the first puppy appears. Again do not try to help. The bitch will eat the placenta from each pup as it is born, licking the pup clean and dry. However, if the bitch has more than five pups do not let her eat all the placentas which, though nutritious can cause diarrhoea if eaten in too great a quantity.

Remember, whelping is not a show and it is absolutely imperative that the bitch gets peace and quiet during delivery. Watching the young of any species being born is always a moving experience and at the time it is tempting to allow all and sundry to peer in, but this really is not fair on the bitch and will make her nervous and upset. So keep curious visitors away and allow only the family to watch from a distance in silence.

As each pup is born, blood and other fluids will dribble out, wetting the newspapers which should be removed gently, giving each pup some clean, dry sheets. Usually puppies are born about one every half hour, though do not be alarmed if it is as much as two hours between pups. As a pup appears you will see it is encased in a thin membrane which the bitch will lick off and eat. However, if the bitch does not free the membrane from around the pup's head it is permissible for you to peel it off, otherwise the pup will be unable to breathe and will die of asphyxia. As I said before you should not normally interfere with the bitch, but if the pups are being delivered quickly the bitch may not be able thoroughly to clean and dry each one. You can then assist by drying with a clean towel any the bitch has missed. If the umbilical cord is still attached nip it off with your finger nails (better even than scissors) about 5cm from the puppy's tummy. Extreme care must be taken to ensure that you do not pull on the cord for such a slip could badly damage the pup's stomach muscles.

If the bitch is obviously still trying to whelp, and no pup appears after about two and a half hours you must summon your vet. Also, if during the delivery a green, bile-like, foul-smelling discharge is exuded from your bitch get the vet immediately. Similarly if you are worried about something which doesn't seem quite right call him in if in doubt. However, be assured that in the vast majority of cases whelping gives few problems and you do not need to interfere in any way. Just be on hand to soothe, comfort and encourage your bitch.

Young puppies

Young puppies need no help at all from you if you have given them a warm, comfortable nest which they cannot stray from. The bitch will look after all their requirements. But remember the bitch herself is dependent on you and you must give her as much good, high-protein food (liver, meat and fish) as desired, in frequent meals. Give her plenty of milk and raw eggs (not more than two a day) for a period of six weeks. Do not try to feed your bitch on the cheap. It is really well worth the extra expense for then not only will the bitch quickly regain condition, but also the pups will benefit from the quality of their mother's feeding.

Dew claw removal
Most puppies are born with what is a rudimentary thumb – an extra claw on the inside of the foreleg, and some even have them on their hind legs as well. If these are not removed they can cause problems in later life, catching on every conceivable object. The other problem is, of course, that since the dew claw is never in contact with the ground it is not worn down and will need paring to prevent it growing in a full circle back into the dog's leg. It is a very simple operation to remove them, normally done between three and five days old, but must be done by your vet.

Tail docking
The business of tail docking should be made clear in an unemotional fashion. For years discussion has been batted backwards and forwards on the advantages and disadvantages of this practice. One side claims that this is unnecessary mutilation, while the other asserts that docking avoids injury to the animal from thorns, barbed wire, etc. My own opinion is that basically it is fashion which dictates that certain dogs should have portions of their tails removed, and in most breeds I believe this to be utterly unnecessary. It seems ridiculous to me to claim that tail docking prevents injury when in the case of German pointers for instance very little of their tail is removed, and springer spaniels, whose tails are thick, well covered in hair and 'flagged', have only the last one-third removed. Certainly a spaniel with an undocked tail is more liable to pick up debris and put the owner to the inconvenience of cleaning it and brushing it out, but most tail docking is really unnecessary.

However, if you wish to have your puppies' tails docked I would advise you to go to a vet, though it can be done at home.

For those who insist on doing it themselves, the method is fairly simple and should be carried out when the puppies are four days old. Get an extremely sharp kitchen cleaver or heavy carving knife and heat the cutting edge over your cooker or bottled gas flame until it is hot enough to singe newspaper. With the assistance of a friend put the puppy on a table with its tail on a carving board. Let your friend hold the puppy, put the tip of the blade on the board with the tail below the blade and draw the knife down in one sharp, forceful movement through the joints of the tail. The hot metal will cauterise the tiny blood vessels and prevent bleeding. If blood appears another gentle touch with the hot blade on the wound will stop it. Re-heat the knife for each puppy. However, unless you are experienced with this operation you would be unwise to attempt it yourself.

Worming

All puppies are born with worms in their intestines, and it is imperative that you worm each pup at the age of four weeks, otherwise these nasty parasites will thrive in the puppy's intestines, living on the proteins in the stomach, and the puppy will quickly lose condition. There are a number of puppy worming treatments you can buy, though once again I recommend that you procure them from your vet.

Claw trimming

At about the age of four weeks suckling puppies can develop needle-sharp little claws which, as they are pushing at the bitch's abdomen, can scratch. If you see the bitch is really uncomfortable when feeding, getting jagged and scratched, you will obviously want to do something about this. However, should you attempt to trim the puppies' claws, it must be done with great delicacy. You will see that each claw has a tiny, sharp tip. That is all you must cut, the very tip. Any heavy-handed action, cutting it too far up for instance, could cut into the quick, which is extremely painful. It is comparatively easy to see the quick inside the claw when the dog has white claws, since the claws are normally opalescent, and the little pink core is visible. It is cutting this which must be avoided at all costs.

Weaning

Generally speaking puppies should be given additional food at the age of about three weeks. Unlike cats, puppies must learn to lap, and this is done by gently dipping their mouths into a saucer of milk. They will lick their muzzles, enjoy the taste and soon start to lap. You can also encourage them by dipping your finger in the milk and letting them lick it off.

At that age two small meals a day are sufficient, and these should be made up of milky drinks and cereals. Baby food is excellent. Gradually increase the number of feeds to six a day at the age of six weeks. You can start giving the puppies a little meat, preferably cooked, mixed with cereal when they are five to six weeks old, and a raw egg whisked into the milk is also good for them.

The bitch's milk should gradually dry up as the puppies feed less and less from her, and at the age of seven to eight weeks they should be completely weaned. Try to discourage persistent pups from suckling their mother after that time to allow the bitch's lactation to cease completely.

Selling the puppies

If you have puppies it is advisable that you advertise them for sale as soon as they are born, taking orders from likely purchasers, since it gives you approximately two months in which to place them in good homes. Do not remove the pups until they are eight weeks old, and certainly not all at once. That could be very distressing for the bitch and it is generally much better to spread the removal over several days or even a couple of weeks.

Make sure that you give a hand-written and signed copy of each puppy's pedigree to the new owner, and have it ready to give out as each puppy is bought. It is not good form to make the purchaser wait for weeks for you to 'get around to' sending the pedigree on to him. Pedigree forms can be easily obtained from pet shops, meal stores, or veterinary surgeries.

11
Your dog's future

In the years ahead it is wise to remember that you must keep your dog in practice and not fall into the trap of thinking that once he is trained you can relax at the end of each shooting season with the intention of giving a short brush-up before the opening of the following season, because it won't work. As your dog matures, if you employ some simple tactics you will greatly assist his mental development, working out problems and retaining alertness. It is not a bad thing occasionally to take your dog into the training field and go through a full training period again, enforcing discipline and speed, and cementing your working relationship.

The sort of thing I do, even with my very experienced middle-aged dog, is to go out early in the day and place a number of hidden decoys, thrown well into cover, over walls, in the edges of streams, and any other difficult locations I can dream up. I will then take the dog out to the same area a little later, as though for an exercising walk. When I am perhaps 60m from the first decoy I will call the dog in and direct him out on a totally cold and blind retrieve. With some dogs it may help if you fire your starting pistol when the dog is turned away from you. This will quickly give him the idea that work is about to commence.

After I have taken the first retrieve I will then work the dog onto each consecutive hidden decoy from greater and greater distances, finally pushing out to 150m or so. Remember that the dog has no indication of where to start hunting, and he can only use the wind to carry scent, and my command for general direction. This is a particularly good test for me as well as the dog which should be fully capable of dropping when told to from as far as he can hear my whistle and take hand signals.

I find older dogs not used for trialing (with their subsequent more rigorous and regular training) tend to get a bit cocky, inventing a distance barrier beyond which they are outside your control. This should never be allowed to happen for there is great pleasure to be had in working your dog far out on a cold, unseen retrieve. You will find that as your dog develops understanding and self-confidence in his interpretation of your commands that you should be able to put out very far-thrown dummies, and with one hand signal alone send him swiftly off to retrieve.

This business of understanding, control, and self-confidence is possibly best explained in the following incident. Occasionally I take my black labrador, Bracken, stalking with me. Although he has obviously no part to play on such a trip I take him on the hill because this provides good exercise under control.

Once I was stalking a large stag. As usual when I started the stalk I put the dog on hup using a hand signal only, and crawled off after the stag. As I reached the position where I intended to take the shot I was just in time to see the beast disappearing around the corner of the hill 200m further on. Quickly I scuttled after it and cautiously crawled around the hill. The beast was still about 100m away. I took aim and dropped the stag.

At the sound of the shot, another fine beast, which I had not seen before, stood up out of the long heather, and I shot it as well. I hurried down the hill and gralloched both deer. I was half-way through gralloching the second one when I realised I had left Bracken behind on the hill, so I walked back to him. The dog was still exactly where I left him, casually lying in the heather coolly and confidently watching for me. Bracken had been left alone for over half an hour during which time there were two loud rifle shots which to the dog signalled titbits of liver as I performed the gralloch. Yet the dog's total confidence in himself and me had enabled him to resist the temptation to creep forward to join the action. When I reappeared I made one hand motion and Bracken came tearing toward me. That is the sort of discipline and understanding that you should try to achieve.

Remember that working dogs can get frustrated in adult life if they are not kept in business so you must endeavour to keep your dog on his toes. As I have already said, over the years the dog will gain a great deal of experience as he matures, and while I am in no way suggesting that you drop your discipline, it is essential that you recognise your dog's character and personality. So it is permissible to relax a little, since after all the dog is not a machine. Most will get to know fairly quickly the difference between work and play. My own dogs for instance will romp about like puppies, play with my children, run about the beach, leap in and out of boats, and act as general pets and companions, yet when the time comes for work they will slot into that groove with no trouble at all.

If you look after your dog and keep him comfortable, feed him a good diet with occasional changes, groom him, and give him love, he will work his heart out for you and truly be your friend.

Index

Figures in **bold** type refer to illustrations